Nimphidia & Other Poems by Michael Drayton

Michael Drayton was born in 1563 at Hartshill, near Nuneaton, Warwickshire, England. The facts of his early life remain unknown.

Drayton first published, in 1590, a volume of spiritual poems; The Harmony of the Church. Ironically the Archbishop of Canterbury seized almost the entire edition and had it destroyed.

In 1593 he published Idea: The Shepherd's Garland, 9 pastorals celebrating his own love-sorrows under the poetic name of Rowland. This was later expanded to a 64 sonnet cycle.

With the publication of The Legend of Piers Gaveston, Matilda and Mortimeriados, later enlarged and re-published, in 1603, under the title of The Barons' Wars. His career began to gather interest and attention.

In 1596, The Legend of Robert, Duke of Normandy, another historical poem was published, followed in 1597 by England's Heroical Epistles, a series of historical studies, in imitation of those of Ovid. Written in the heroic couplet, they contain some of his finest writing.

Like other poets of his era, Drayton wrote for the theatre; but unlike Shakespeare, Jonson, or Samuel Daniel, he invested little of his art in the genre. Between 1597 and 1602, Drayton was a member of the stable of playwrights who worked for Philip Henslowe. Henslowe's Diary links Drayton's name with 23 plays from that period, and, for all but one unfinished work, in collaboration with others such as Thomas Dekker, Anthony Munday, and Henry Chettle. Only one play has survived; Part 1 of Sir John Oldcastle, which Drayton wrote with Munday, Robert Wilson, and Richard Hathwaye but little of Drayton can be seen in its pages.

By this time, as a poet, Drayton was well received and admired at the Court of Elizabeth 1st. If he hoped to continue that admiration with the accession of James 1st he thought wrong. In 1603, he addressed a poem of compliment to James I, but it was ridiculed, and his services rudely rejected.

In 1605 Drayton reprinted his most important works; the historical poems and the Idea. Also published was a fantastic satire called The Man in the Moon and, for the for the first time the famous Ballad of Agincourt.

Since 1598 he had worked on Poly-Olbion, a work to celebrate all the points of topographical or antiquarian interest in Great Britain. Eighteen books in total, the first were published in 1614 and the last in 1622.

In 1627 he published another of his miscellaneous volumes. In it Drayton printed The Battle of Agincourt (an historical poem but not to be confused with his ballad on the same subject), The Miseries of Queen Margaret, and the acclaimed Nimphidia, the Court of Faery, as well as several other important pieces.

Drayton last published in 1630 with The Muses' Elizium.

Michael Drayton died in London on December 23rd, 1631. He was buried in Westminster Abbey, in Poets' Corner. A monument was placed there with memorial lines attributed to Ben Jonson.

Index of Contents

NIMPHIDIA

THE COURT OF FAYRIE

Olde CHAUCER doth of Topas tell,
Mad RABLAIS of Pantagruell,
A latter third of Dowsabell,
With such poore trifles playing:
Others the like have laboured at
Some of this thing, and some of that,
And many of they know not what,
But that they must be saying.

Another sort there bee, that will
Be talking of the Fayries still,
Nor never can they have their fill,
As they were wedded to them;
No Tales of them their thirst can slake,
So much delight therein they take,
And some strange thing they fame would make,
Knew they the way to doe them.

Then since no Muse hath bin so bold,
Or of the Later, or the ould,
Those Eluish secrets to unfold,
Which lye from others reading,
My actiue Muse to light shall bring,
The court of that proud Fayry King,
And tell there, of the Reuelling,
Love prosper my proceeding.

And thou NIMPHIDIA gentle Fay,
Which meeting me upon the way,
These secrets didst to me bewray,
Which now I am in telling:
My pretty light fantastick mayde,
I here inuoke thee to my ayde,
That I may speake what thou hast sayd,
In numbers smoothly swelling.

This Pallace standeth in the Ayre,
By Nigromancie placed there,
That it no Tempests needs to feare,
Which way so ere it blow it.
And somewhat Southward tow'rd the Noone,
Whence lyes a way up to the Moone,
And thence the Fayrie can as soone
Passe to the earth below it.

The Walls of Spiders legs are made,
Well mortized and finely layd,
He was the master of his Trade
It curiously that builded:
The Windowes of the eyes of Cats,
And for the Roofe, instead of Slats,
Is cover'd with the skinns of Batts,
With Mooneshine that are guilded.

Hence Oberon him sport to make,
(Their rest when weary mortalls take)
And none but onely Fayries wake,
Desendeth for his pleasure.
And Mab his meerry Queene by night
Bestrids young Folks that lye upright,
(In elder Times the Mare that hight)
Which plagues them out of measure.

Hence Shaddowes, seeming Idle shapes,
Of little frisking Elues and Apes,
To Earth doe make their wanton skapes,
As hope of pastime hasts them:
Which maydes think on the Hearth they see,

When Fyers well nere consumed be,
Their daunsing Hayes by two and three,
Iust as their Fancy casts them.

These make our Girles their sluttery rue,
By pinching them both blacke and blew,
And put a penny in their shue,
The house for cleanely sweeping:
And in their courses make that Round,
In Meadowes, and in Marshes found,
Of them so call'd the Fayrie ground,
Of which they have the keeping.

Thus when a Childe haps to be gott,
Which after prooues an Ideott,
When Folke perceiue it thriueth not,
The fault therein to smother:
Some silly doting brainlesse Calfe,
That understands things by the halfe,
Say that the Fayrie left this Aulfe,
And tooke away the other.

But listen and I shall you tell,
A chance in Fayrie that befell,
Which certainly may please some well;
In Love and Armes delighting:
Of Oberon that Iealous grewe,
Of one of his owne Fayrie crue,
Too well (he fear'd) his Queene that knew,
His love but ill requiting.

Pigwiggen was this Fayrie knight,
One wondrous gratious in the sight
Of faire Queene Mab, which day and night,
He amorously obserued;
Which made king Oberon suspect,
His Service tooke too good effect,
His saucinesse, and often checkt,
And could have wisht him starued.

Pigwiggen gladly would commend,
Some token to queene Mab to send,
If Sea, or Land, him ought could lend,
Were worthy of her wearing:
At length this Lover doth devise,
A Bracelett made of Emmotts eyes,
A thing he thought that shee would prize,
No whitt her state impayring.

And to the Queene a Letter writes,
Which he most curiously endites,

Conjuring her by all the rites
Of love, she would be pleased,
To meete him her true Servant, where
They might without suspect or feare,
Themselves to one another cleare,
And have their poore hearts eased.

At mid-night the appointed hower,
And for the Queene a fitting bower,
(Quoth he) is that faire Cowslip flower,
On Hipcut hill that groweth,
In all your Trayne there's not a Fay,
That ever went to gather May,
But she hath made it in her way,
The tallest there that groweth.

When by Tom Thum a Fayrie Page,
He sent it, and doth him engage,
By promise of a mighty wage,
It secretly to carrie:
Which done, the Queene her maydes doth call,
And bids them to be ready all,
She would goe see her Summer Hall,
She could no longer tarrie.

Her Chariot ready straight is made,
Each thing therein is fitting layde,
That she by nothing might be stayde,
For naught must be her letting,
Foure nimble Gnats the Horses were,
Their Harnasses of Gossamere,
Flye Cranion her Chariottere,
Upon the Coach-box getting.

Her Chariot of a Snayles fine shell,
Which for the colours did excell:
The faire Queene Mab, becomming well,
So lively was the limming:
The seate the soft wooll of the Bee;
The cover, (gallantly to see)
The wing of a pyde Butterflee,
I trowe t'was simple trimming.

The wheeles compos'd of Crickets bones,
And daintily made for the nonce,
For feare of ratling on the stones,
With Thistle-downe they shod it;
For all her Maydens much did feare,
If Oberon had chanc'd to heare,
That Mab his Queene should have bin there,
He would not have aboad it.

She mounts her Chariot with a trice,
Nor would she stay for no advice,
Untill her Maydes that were so nice,
To wayte on her were fitted,
But ranne her selfe away alone;
Which when they heard there was not one,
But hasted after to be gone,
As she had beene diswitted.

Hop, and Mop, and Drop so cleare,
Pip, and Trip, and Skip that were,
To Mab their Soveraigne ever deare:
Her speciall Maydes of Honour;
Fib, and Tib, and Pinck, and Pin,
Tick, and Quick, and Iill, and Iin,
Tit, and Nit, and Wap, and Win,
The Trayne that wayte upon her.

Upon a Grasshopper they got,
And what with Amble, and with Trot,
For hedge nor ditch they spared not,
But after her they hie them.
A Cobweb over them they throw,
To shield the winde if it should blowe,
Themselves they wisely could bestowe,
Lest any should espie them.

But let us leaue Queene Mab a while,
Through many a gate, o'r many a stile,
That now had gotten by this wile,
Her deare Pigwiggin kissing,
And tell how Oberon doth fare,
Who grew as mad as any Hare,
When he had sought each place with care,
And found his Queene was missing.

By grisly Pluto he doth sweare,
He rent his cloths, and tore his haire,
And as he runneth, here and there,
An Acorne cup he greeteth;
Which soone he taketh by the stalke
About his head he lets it walke,
Nor doth he any creature balke,
But lays on all he meeteth.

The Thuskan Poet doth advance,
The franticke Paladine of France,
And those more ancient doe inhaunce,
Alcides in his fury.
And others Aiax Telamon,

But to this time there hath bin non,
So Bedlam as our Oberon,
Of which I dare assure you.

And first encountring with a waspe,
He in his armes the Fly doth claspe
As though his breath he forth would graspe,
Him for Pigwiggen taking:
Where is my wife thou Rogue, quoth he,
Pigwiggen, she is come to thee,
Restore her, or thou dy'st by me,
Whereat the poore waspe quaking,

Cryes, Oberon, great Fayrie King,
Content thee I am no such thing,
I am a Waspe behold my sting,
At which the Fayrie started:
When soone away the Waspe doth goe,
Poore wretch was never frighted so,
He thought his wings were much to slow,
O'rjoyd, they so were parted.

He next upon a Glow-worme light,
(You must suppose it now was night),
Which for her hinder part was bright,
He tooke to be a Devill.
And furiously doth her assaile
For carrying fier in her taile
He thrasht her rough coat with his flayle,
The mad King fear'd no euill.

O quoth the Gloworme hold thy hand,
Thou puisant King of Fayrie land,
Thy mighty stroaks who may withstand,
Hould, or of life despaire I:
Together then her selfe doth roule,
And tumbling downe into a hole,
She seem'd as black as any Cole,
Which vext away the Fayrie.

From thence he ran into a Hive,
Amongst the Bees he letteth drive
And downe their Coombes begins to rive,
All likely to have spoyled:
Which with their Waxe his face besmeard,
And with their Honey daub'd his Beard
It would have made a man afeard,
To see how he was moyled.

A new Aduenture him betides,
He mett an Ant, which he bestrides,

And post thereon away he rides,
Which with his haste doth stumble;
And came full over on her snowte,
Her heels so threw the dirt about,
For she by no meanes could get out,
But over him doth tumble.

And being in this piteous case,
And all be-slurried head and face,
On runs he in this Wild-goose chase
As here, and there, he rambles
Halfe blinde, against a molehill hit,
And for a Mountaine taking it,
For all he was out of his wit,
Yet to the top he scrambles.

And being gotten to the top,
Yet there himselfe he could not stop,
But downe on th' other side doth chop,
And to the foot came rumbling:
So that the Grubs therein that bred,
Hearing such turmoyle over head,
Thought surely they had all bin dead,
So fearefull was the lumbling.

And falling downe into a Lake,
Which him up to the neck doth take,
His fury somewhat it doth slake,
He calleth for a Ferry;
Where you may some recovery note,
What was his Club he made his Boate,
And in his Oaken Cup doth float,
As safe as in a Wherry.

Men talke of the Aduentures strange,
Of Don Quishott, and of their change
Through which he Armed oft did range,
Of Sancha Panchas travell:
But should a man tell every thing,
Done by this franticke Fayrie king.
And them in lofty numbers sing
It well his wits might grauell.

Scarse set on shore, but therewithall,
He meeteth Pucke, which most men call
Hobgoblin, and on him doth fall,
With words from frenzy spoken;
Hoh, hoh, quoth Hob, God saue thy grace,
Who drest thee in this pitteous case,
He thus that spoild my soveraignes face,
I would his necke were broken.

This Puck seemes but a dreaming dolt,
Still walking like a ragged Colt,
And oft out of a Bush doth bolt,
Of purpose to deceiue us.
And leading us makes us to stray,
Long Winters nights out of the way,
And when we stick in mire and clay,
Hob doth with laughter leaue us.

Deare Puck (quoth he) my wife is gone
As ere thou lou'st King Oberon,
Let every thing but this alone
With vengeance, and pursue her;
Bring her to me alive or dead,
Or that vilde thief, Pigwiggins head,
That villaine hath defil'd my bed
He to this folly drew her.

Quoth Puck, My Liege Ile never lin,
But I will thorough thicke and thinne,
Untill at length I bring her in,
My dearest Lord nere doubt it:
Thorough Brake, thorough Brier,
Thorough Muck, thorough Mier,
Thorough Water, thorough Fier,
And thus goes Puck about it.

This thing Nimphidia over hard
That on this mad King had a guard
Not doubting of a great reward,
For first this businesse broching;
And through the ayre away doth goe
Swift as an Arrow from the Bowe,
To let her Soveraigne Mab to know,
What perill was approaching.

The Queene bound with Loves powerfulst charme
Sate with Pigwiggen arme in arme,
Her Merry Maydes that thought no harme,
About the roome were skipping:
A Humble-Bee their Minstrell, playde
Upon his Hoboy; eu'ry Mayde
Fit for this Reuells was arayde,
The Hornepype neatly tripping.

In comes Nimphidia, and doth crie,
My Soveraigne for your safety flie,
For there is danger but too nie,
I posted to forewarne you:
The King hath sent Hobgoblin out,

To seeke you all the Fields about,
And of your safety you may doubt,
If he but once discerne you.

When like an uprore in a Towne,
Before them every thing went downe,
Some tore a Ruffe, and some a Gowne,
Gainst one another justling:
They flewe about like Chaffe i' th winde,
For hast some left their Maskes behinde;
Some could not stay their Gloves to finde,
There never was such bustling.

Forth ranne they by a secret way,
Into a brake that neere them lay;
Yet much they doubted there to stay,
Lest Hob should hap to find them:
He had a sharpe and piercing sight,
All one to him the day and night,
And therefore were resolu'd by flight,
To leave this place behind them.

At length one chanc'd to find a Nut,
In th' end of which a hole was cut,
Which lay upon a Hazell roote,
There scatt'red by a Squirill:
Which out the kernell gotten had;
When quoth this Fay deare Queene be glad,
Let Oberon be ne'r so mad,
Ile set you safe from perill.

Come all into this Nut (quoth she)
Come closely in be rul'd by me,
Each one may here a chuser be,
For roome yee need not wrastle:
Nor neede yee be together heapt;
So one by one therein they crept,
And lying downe they soundly slept,
And safe as in a Castle.

Nimphidia that this while doth watch,
Perceiu'd if Puck the Queene should catch
That he should be her over-match,
Of which she well bethought her;
Found it must be some powerfull Charme,
The Queene against him that must arme,
Or surely he would doe her harme,
For throughly he had sought her.

And listning if she ought could heare,
That her might hinder, or might feare:

But finding still the coast was cleare,
Nor creature had discride her;
Each circumstance and having scand,
She came thereby to understand,
Puck would be with them out of hand
When to her Charmes she hide her:

And first her Ferne seede doth bestowe,
The kernell of the Missletowe:
And here and there as Puck should goe,
With terrour to affright him:
She Night-shade strawes to work him ill,
Therewith her Veruayne and her Dill,
That hindreth Witches of their will,
Of purpose to dispight him.

Then sprinkles she the iuice of Rue,
That groweth underneath the Yeu:
With nine drops of the midnight dewe,
From Lunarie distilling:
The Molewarps braine mixt therewithall;
And with the same the Pismyres gall,
For she in nothing short would fall;
The Fayrie was so willing.

Then thrice under a Bryer doth creepe,
Which at both ends was rooted deepe,
And over it three times shee leepe;
Her Magicke much avayling:
Then on Proserpyna doth call,
And so upon her spell doth fall,
Which here to you repeate I shall,
Not in one tittle fayling.

By the croking of the Frogge;
By the howling of the Dogge;
By the crying of the Hogge,
Against the storme arising;
By the Euening Curphewe bell;
By the dolefull dying knell,
O let this my direfull Spell,
Hob, hinder thy surprising.

By the Mandrakes dreadfull groanes;
By the Lubricans sad moans;
By the noyse of dead mens bones,
In Charnell houses ratling:
By the hissing of the Snake,
The rustling of the fire-Drake,
I charge thee thou this place forsake,
Nor of Queene Mab be pratling.

By the Whirlwindes hollow sound,
By the Thunders dreadfull stound,
Yells of Spirits under ground,
I chardge thee not to feare us:
By the Shreech-owles dismall note,
By the Blacke Night-Ravens throate,
I charge thee Hob to teare thy Coate
With thornes if thou come neere us,

Her Spell thus spoke she stept aside,
And in a Chincke her selfe doth hide,
To see there of what would betyde,
For shee doth onely minde him:
When presently shee Puck espies,
And well she markt his gloating eyes,
How under every leafe he spies,
In seeking still to finde them.

But once the Circle got within,
The Charmes to worke doe straight begin,
And he was caught as in a Gin;
For as he thus was busie,
A paine he in his Head-peece feeles,
Against a stubbed Tree he reeles,
And up went poore Hobgoblins heeles,
Alas his braine was dizzie.

At length upon his feete he gets,
Hobgoblin fumes, Hobgoblin frets,
And as againe he forward sets,
And through the Bushes scrambles;
A Stump doth trip him in his pace,
Down comes poore Hob upon his face,
And lamentably tore his case,
Amongst the Bryers and Brambles.

A plague upon Queene Mab, quoth hee,
And all her Maydes where ere they be,
I thinke the Deuill guided me,
To seeke her so provoked.
Where stumbling at a piece of Wood,
He fell into a dich of mudd,
Where to the very Chin he stood,
In danger to be choked.

Now worse than e're he was before:
Poore Puck doth yell, poore Puck doth rore;
That wak'd Queene Mab who doubted sore
Some Treason had been wrought her:
Untill Nimphidia told the Queene

What she had done, what she had seene,
Who then had well-neere crack'd her spleene
With very extreame laughter.

But leaue we Hob to clamber out:
Queene Mab and all her Fayrie rout,
And come againe to have about
With Oberon yet madding:
And with Pigwiggen now distrought,
Who much was troubled in his thought,
That he so long the Queene had sought,
And through the Fields was gadding.

And as he runnes he still doth crie,
King Oberon I thee defie,
And dare thee here in Armes to trie,
For my deare Ladies honour:
For that she is a Queene right good,
In whose defence Ile shed my blood,
And that thou in this iealous mood
Hast lay'd this slander on her.

And quickly Armes him for the Field,
A little Cockle-shell his Shield,
Which he could very bravely wield:
Yet could it not be pierced:
His Speare a Bent both stiffe and strong,
And well-neere of two Inches long;
The Pyle was of a Horse-flyes tongue,
Whose sharpnesse nought reversed.

And puts him on a coate of Male,
Which was of a Fishes scale,
That when his Foe should him assaile,
No poynt should be prevayling:
His Rapier was a Hornets sting,
It was a very dangerous thing:
For if he chanc'd to hurt the King,
It would be long in healing.

His Helmet was a Bettles head,
Most horrible and full of dread,
That able was to strike one dead,
Yet did it well become him:
And for a plume, a horses hayre,
Which being tossed with the ayre,
Had force to strike his Foe with feare,
And turne his weapon from him.

Himselfe he on an Earewig set,
Yet scarce he on his back could get,

So oft and high he did coruet,
Ere he himselfe could settle:
He made him turne, and stop, and bound,
To gallop, and to trot the Round,
He scarce could stand on any ground,
He was so full of mettle.

When soone he met with Tomalin,
One that a valiant Knight had bin,
And to King Oberon of kin;
Quoth he thou manly Fayrie:
Tell Oberon I come prepar'd,
Then bid him stand upon his Guard;
This hand his basenesse shall reward,
Let him be ne'r so wary.

Say to him thus, that I defie,
His slanders, and his infamie,
And as a mortall enemie,
Doe publickly proclaime him:
Withall, that if I had mine owne,
He should not weare the Fayrie Crowne,
But with a vengeance should come downe:
Nor we a King should name him.

This Tomalin could not abide,
To heare his Soveraigne vilefide:
But to the Fayrie Court him hide;
Full furiously he posted,
With eu'ry thing Pigwiggen sayd:
How title to the Crowne he layd,
And in what Armes he was aray'd,
As how himselfe he boasted.

Twixt head and foot, from point to point,
He told th'arming of each joint,
In every piece, how neate, and quaint,
For Tomalin could doe it:
How fayre he sat, how sure he rid,
As of the courser he bestrid,
How Mannag'd, and how well he did;
The King which listened to it,

Quoth he, goe Tomalin with speede,
Provide me Armes, provide my Steed,
And every thing that I shall neede,
By thee I will be guided;
To strait account, call thou thy witt,
See there be wanting not a whitt,
In every thing see thou me fitt,
Just as my foes provided.

Soone flewe this newes through Fayrie land
Which gave Queene Mab to understand,
The combate that was then in hand,
Betwixt those men so mighty:
Which greatly she began to rew,
Perceuing that all Fayrie knew,
The first occasion from her grew,
Of these affaires so weighty.

Wherefore attended with her maides,
Through fogs, and mists, and dampes she wades,
To Proserpine the Queene of shades
To treat, that it would please her,
The cause into her hands to take,
For ancient love and friendships sake,
And soone therof an end to make,
Which of much care would ease her.

A While, there let we Mab alone,
And come we to King Oberon,
Who arm'd to meete his foe is gone,
For Proud Pigwiggen crying:
Who sought the Fayrie King as fast,
And had so well his iourneyes cast,
That he arriued at the last,
His puisant foe espying:

Stout Tomalin came with the King,
Tom Thum doth on Pigwiggen bring,
That perfect were in every thing,
To single fights belonging:
And therefore they themselves ingage,
To see them exercise their rage,
With faire and comely equipage,
Not one the other wronging.

So like in armes, these champions were,
As they had bin, a very paire,
So that a man would almost sweare,
That either, had bin either;
Their furious steedes began to naye
That they were heard a mighty way,
Their staues upon their rests they lay;
Yet e'r they flew together,

Their Seconds minister an oath,
Which was indifferent to them both,
That on their Knightly faith, and troth,
No magicke them supplyed;
And sought them that they had no charmes,

Wherewith to worke each others harmes,
But came with simple open armes,
To have their causes tryed.

Together furiously they ran,
That to the ground came horse and man,
The blood out of their Helmets span,
So sharpe were their incounters;
And though they to the earth were throwne,
Yet quickly they regain'd their owne,
Such nimblenesse was never showne,
They were two Gallant Mounters.

When in a second Course againe,
They forward came with might and mayne,
Yet which had better of the twaine,
The Seconds could not judge yet;
Their shields were into pieces cleft,
Their helmets from their heads were reft,
And to defend them nothing left,
These Champions would not budge yet.

Away from them their Staues they threw,
Their cruell Swords they quickly drew,
And freshly they the fight renew;
They every stroke redoubled:
Which made Proserpina take heed,
And make to them the greater speed,
For fear lest they too much should bleed,
Which wondrously her troubled.

When to th' infernall Stix she goes,
She takes the Fogs from thence that rose,
And in a Bagge doth them enclose;
When well she had them blended:
She hyes her then to Lethe spring,
A Bottell and thereof doth bring,
Wherewith she meant to worke the thing,
Which onely she intended.

Now Proserpine with Mab is gone
Unto the place where Oberon
And proud Pigwiggen, one to one,
Both to be slaine were likely:
And there themselves they closely hide,
Because they would not be espide;
For Proserpine meant to decide
The matter very quickly.

And suddainly untyes the Poke,
Which out of it sent such a smoke,

As ready was them all to choke,
So greeuous was the pother;
So that the Knights each other lost,
And stood as still as any post,
Tom Thum, nor Tomalin could boast
Themselves of any other.

But when the mist gan somewhat cease,
Proserpina commanded peace:
And that a while they should release,
Each other of their perill:
Which here (quoth she) I doe proclaime
To all in dreadfull Plutos name,
That as yee will eschewe his blame,
You let me heare the quarrell,

But here your selves you must engage,
Somewhat to coole your spleenish rage:
Your greeuous thirst and to asswage,
That first you drinke this liquor:
Which shall your understanding cleare,
As plainely shall to you appeare;
Those things from me that you shall heare,
Conceiving much the quicker.

This Lethe water you must knowe,
The memory destroyeth so,
That of our weale, or of our woe,
It all remembrance blotted;
Of it nor can you ever thinke:
For they no sooner tooke this drinke,
But nought into their braines could sinke,
Of what had them besotted.

King Oberon forgotten had,
That he for iealousie ranne mad:
But of his Queene was wondrous glad,
And ask'd how they came thither:
Pigwiggen likewise doth forget,
That he Queene Mab had ever met;
Or that they were so hard beset,
When they were found together.

Nor neither of them both had thought,
That e'r they had each other sought;
Much lesse that they a Combat fought,
But such a dreame were lothing:
Tom Thum had got a little sup,
And Tomalin scarce kist the Cup,
Yet had their braines so sure lockt up,
That they remembred nothing.

Queene Mab and her light Maydes the while,
Amongst themselves doe closely smile,
To see the King caught with this wile,
With one another testing:
And to the Fayrie Court they went,
With mickle joy and merriment,
Which thing was done with good intent,
And thus I left them feasting.

THE QUEST OF CYNTHIA

What time the groves were clad in greene,
The Fields drest all in flowers,
And that the sleeke-hayred Nimphs were seene,
To seeke them Summer Bowers.

Forth rou'd I by the sliding Rills,
To finde where CYNTHIA sat,
Whose name so often from the hills,
The Ecchos wondred at.

When me upon my Quest to bring,
That pleasure might excell,
The Birds stroue which should sweetliest sing,
The Flowers which sweet'st should smell.

Long wand'ring in the Woods (said I)
Oh whether's CYNTHIA gone?
When soone the Eccho doth reply,
To my last word, goe on.

At length upon a lofty Firre,
It was my chance to finde,
Where that deare name most due to her,
Was caru'd upon the rynde.

Which whilst with wonder I beheld,
The Bees their hony brought,
And up the carued letters fild,
As they with gould were wrought.

And neere that trees more spacious roote,
Then looking on the ground,
The shape of her most dainty foot,
Imprinted there I found.

Which stuck there like a curious seale,
As though it should forbid

Us, wretched mortalls, to reueale,
What under it was hid.

Besides the flowers which it had pres'd,
Apeared to my vew,
More fresh and lovely than the rest,
That in the meadowes grew:

The cleere drops in the steps that stood,
Of that dilicious Girle,
The Nimphes amongst their dainty food,
Drunke for dissolued pearle.

The yeilding sand, where she had troad,
Untutcht yet with the winde,
By the faire posture plainely show'd,
Where I might Cynthia finde.

When on upon my waylesse walke,
As my desires me draw,
I like a madman fell to talke,
With every thing I saw:

I ask'd some Lillyes why so white,
They from their fellowes were;
Who answered me, that Cynthia's sight,
Had made them looke so cleare:

I ask'd a nodding Violet why,
It sadly hung the head,
It told me Cynthia late past by,
Too soone from it that fled:

A bed of Roses saw I there,
Bewitching with their grace:
Besides so wondrous sweete they were,
That they perfum'd the place,

I of a Shrube of those enquir'd,
From others of that kind,
Who with such virtue them enspir'd,
It answer'd (to my minde).

As the base Hemblocke were we such,
The poysned'st weed that growes,
Till Cynthia by her god-like tuch,
Transform'd us to the Rose:

Since when those Frosts that winter brings
Which candy every greene,
Renew us like the Teeming Springs,

And we thus Fresh are scene.

At length I on a Fountaine light,
Whose brim with Pincks was platted;
The Banck with Daffadillies dight,
With grasse like Sleaue was matted,

When I demanded of that Well,
What power frequented there;
Desiring, it would please to tell
What name it usde to beare.

It tolde me it was Cynthias owne,
Within whose cheerefull brimmes,
That curious Nimph had oft beene knowne
To bath her snowy Limmes.

Since when that Water had the power,
Lost Mayden-heads to restore,
And make one Twenty in an howre,
Of Esons age before.

And told me that the bottome cleere,
Now layd with many a fett
Of seed-pearle, ere shee bath'd her there:
Was knowne as blacke as Jet,

As when she from the water came,
Where first she touch'd the molde,
In balls the people made the same
For Pomander, and solde.

When chance me to an Arbour led,
Whereas I might behold:
Two blest Elizeums in one sted,
The lesse the great enfold.

The place which she had chosen out,
Her selfe in to repose;
Had they com'n downe, the gods no doubt
The very same had chose.

The wealthy Spring yet never bore
That sweet, nor dainty flower
That damask'd not, the chequer'd flore
Of CYNTHIAS Summer Bower.

The Birch, the Mirtle, and the Bay,
Like Friends did all embrace;
And their large branches did display,
To Canapy the place.

Where she like VENUS doth appeare,
Upon a Rosie bed;
As Lillyes the soft pillowes weare,
Whereon she layd her head.

Heau'n on her shape such cost bestow'd,
And with such bounties blest:
No lim of hers but might have made
A Goddesse at the least.

The Flyes by chance mesht in her hayre,
By the bright Radience throwne
From her cleare eyes, rich Iewels weare,
They so like Diamonds shone.

The meanest weede the soyle there bare,
Her breath did so refine,
That it with Woodbynd durst compare,
And beard the Eglantine.

The dewe which on the tender grasse,
The Euening had distill'd,
To pure Rose-water turned was,
The shades with sweets that fill'd.

The windes were husht, no leafe so small
At all was scene to stirre:
Whilst tuning to the waters fall,
The small Birds sang to her.

Where she too quickly me espies,
When I might plainely see,
A thousand Cupids from her eyes
Shoote all at once at me.

Into these secret shades (quoth she)
How dar'st thou be so bold
To enter, consecrate to me,
Or touch this hallowed mold.

Those words (quoth she) I can pronounce,
Which to that shape can bring
Thee, which the Hunter had who once
Sawe Dian in the Spring.

Bright Nimph againe I thus replie,
This cannot me affright:
I had rather in thy presence die,
Then live out of thy sight.

I first upon the Mountaines hie,
Built Altars to thy name;
And grau'd it on the Rocks thereby,
To propogate thy fame.

I taught the Shepheards on the Downes,
Of thee to frame their Layes:
T'was I that fill'd the neighbouring Townes,
With Ditties of thy praise.

Thy colours I devis'd with care,
Which were unknowne before:
Which since that, in their braded hayre
The Nimphes and Siluans wore.

Transforme me to what shape you can,
I passe not what it be:
Yea what most hatefull is to man,
So I may follow thee.

Which when she heard full pearly floods,
I in her eyes might view:
(Quoth she) most welcome to these Woods,
Too meane for one so true.

Here from the hatefull world we'll live,
A den of mere dispight:
To Ideots only that doth give,
Which be her sole delight.

To people the infernall pit,
That more and more doth strive;
Where only villany is wit,
And Divels only thrive.

Whose vilenesse us shall never awe:
But here our sports shall be:
Such as the golden world first sawe,
Most innocent and free.

Of Simples in these Groves that growe,
Wee'll learne the perfect skill;
The nature of each Herbe to knowe
Which cures, and which can kill.

The waxen Pallace of the Bee,
We seeking will surprise
The curious workmanship to see,
Of her full laden thighes.

Wee'll suck the sweets out of the Combe,

And make the gods repine:
As they doe feast in Joues great roome,
To see with what we dine.

Yet when there haps a honey fall,
Wee'll lick the sirupt leaues:
And tell the Bees that their's is gall,
To this upon the Greaues.

The nimble Squirrell noting here,
Her mossy Dray that makes,
And laugh to see the lusty Deere
Come bounding ore the brakes.

The Spiders Webb to watch weele stand,
And when it takes the Bee,
Weele helpe out of the Tyrants hand,
The Innocent to free.

Sometime weele angle at the Brooke,
The freckled Trout to take,
With silken Wormes, and bayte the hooke,
Which him our prey shall make.

Of medling with such subtile tooles,
Such dangers that enclose,
The Morrall is that painted Fooles,
Are caught with silken showes.

And when the Moone doth once appeare,
Weele trace the lower grounds,
When Fayries in their Ringlets there
Do daunce their nightly rounds.

And have a Flocke of Turtle Doues,
A guard on us to keepe,
A witnesse of our honest loves,
To watch us till we sleepe.

Which spoke I felt such holy fires
To overspred my breast,
As lent life to my Chast desires
And gaue me endlesse rest.

By Cynthia thus doe I subsist,
On earth Heavens onely pride,
Let her be mine, and let who list,
Take all the world beside.

THE SHEPHEARDS SIRENA

DORILUS in sorrowes deepe,
Autumne waxing olde and chill,
As he sate his Flocks to keepe
Underneath an easie hill:
Chanc'd to cast his eye aside
On those fields, where he had scene,
Bright SIRENA Natures pride,
Sporting on the pleasant greene:
To whose walkes the Shepheards oft,
Came her god-like foote to finde,
And in places that were soft,
Kist the print there left behinde;
Where the path which she had troad,
Hath thereby more glory gayn'd,
Then in heau'n that milky rode,
Which with Nectar Hebe stayn'd:
But bleake Winters boystrous blasts,
Now their fading pleasures chid,
And so fill'd them with his wastes,
That from sight her steps were hid.
Silly Shepheard sad the while,
For his sweet SIRENA gone,
All his pleasures in exile:
Layd on the colde earth alone.
Whilst his gamesome cut-tayld Curre,
With his mirthlesse Master playes,
Striuing him with sport to stirre,
As in his more youthfull dayes,
DORILUS his Dogge doth chide,
Layes his well-tun'd Bagpype by,
And his Sheep-hooke casts aside,
There (quoth he) together lye.
When a Letter forth he tooke,
Which to him SIRENA writ,
With a deadly down-cast looke,
And thus fell to reading it.
DORILUS my deare (quoth she)
Kinde Companion of my woe,
Though we thus diuided be,
Death cannot diuorce us so:
Thou whose bosome hath beene still,
Th' onely Closet of my care,
And in all my good and ill,
Ever had thy equall share:
Might I winne thee from thy Fold,
Thou shouldst come to visite me,
But the Winter is so cold,
That I feare to hazard thee:
The wilde waters are waxt hie,

So they are both deafe and dumbe,
Lou'd they thee so well as I,
They would ebbe when thou shouldst come;
Then my coate with light should shine,
Purer then the Vestall fire:
Nothing here but should be thine,
That thy heart can well desire:
Where at large we will relate,
From what cause our friendship grewe,
And in that the varying Fate,
Since we first each other knewe:
Of my heauie passed plight,
As of many a future feare,
Which except the silent night,
None but onely thou shalt heare;
My sad hurt it shall releeue,
When my thoughts I shall disclose,
For thou canst not chuse but greeue,
When I shall recount my woes;
There is nothing to that friend,
To whose close uncranied brest,
We our secret thoughts may send,
And there safely let it rest:
And thy faithfull counsell may,
My distressed case assist,
Sad affliction else may sway
Me a woman as it list:
Hither I would have thee haste,
Yet would gladly have thee stay,
When those dangers I forecast,
That may meet thee by the way,
Doe as thou shalt thinke it best,
Let thy knowledge be thy guide,
Live thou in my constant breast,
Whatsoever shall betide.
He her Letter having red,
Puts it in his Scrip againe,
Looking like a man halfe dead,
By her kindenesse strangely slaine;
And as one who inly knew,
Her distressed present state,
And to her had still been true,
Thus doth with himselfe debate.
I will not thy face admire,
Admirable though it bee,
Nor thine eyes whose subtile fire
So much wonder winne in me:
But my maruell shall be now,
(And of long it hath bene so)
Of all Woman kind that thou
Wert ordain'd to taste of woe;

To a Beauty so divine,
Paradise in little done,
O that Fortune should assigne,
Ought but what thou well mightst shun,
But my counsailes such must bee,
(Though as yet I them conceale)
By their deadly wound in me,
They thy hurt must onely heale,
Could I give what thou do'st crave
To that passe thy state is growne,
I thereby thy life may saue,
But am sure to loose mine owne,
To that joy thou do'st conceiue,
Through my heart, the way doth lye,
Which in two for thee must claue
Least that thou shouldst goe awry.
Thus my death must be a toy,
Which my pensiue breast must cover;
Thy beloved to enjoy,
Must be taught thee by thy Lover.
Hard the Choise I have to chuse,
To my selfe if friend I be,
I must my SIRENA loose,
If not so, shee looseth me.
Thus whilst he doth cast about,
What therein were best to doe,
Nor could yet resolue the doubt,
Whether he should stay or goe:
In those Feilds not farre away,
There was many a frolike Swaine,
In fresh Russets day by day,
That kept Reuells on the Plaine.
Nimble TOM, sirnam'd the Tup,
For his Pipe without a Peere,
And could tickle Trenchmore up,
As t'would joy your heart to heare.
RALPH as much renown'd for skill,
That the Taber touch'd so well;
For his Gittern, little GILL,
That all other did excell.
ROCK and ROLLO every way,
Who still led the Rusticke Ging,
And could troule a Roundelay,
That would make the Feilds to ring,
COLLIN on his Shalme so cleare,
Many a high-pitcht Note that had,
And could make the Eechos nere
Shout as they were wexen mad.
Many a lusty Swaine beside,
That for nought but pleasure car'd,
Having DORILUS espy'd,

And with him knew how it far'd.
Thought from him they would remove,
This strong melancholy fitt,
Or so, should it not behoue,
Quite to put him out of 's witt;
Having learnt a Song, which he
Sometime to Sirena sent,
Full of Iollity and glee,
When the Nimph liu'd neere to Trent
They behinde him softly gott,
Lying on the earth along,
And when he suspected not,
Thus the Iouiall Shepheards song.

Neare to the Silver Trent,
Sirena dwelleth:
Shee to whom Nature lent
All that excelleth:
By which the Muses late,
And the neate Graces,
Have for their greater state
Taken their places:
Twisting an Anadem,
Wherewith to Crowne her,
As it belong'd to them
Most to renowne her.

CHORUS
On thy Bancke,
In a Rancke,
Let the Swanes sing her,
And with their Musick,
Along let them bring her.

Tagus and Pactolus
Are to thee Debter,
Nor for their gould to us
Are they the better:
Henceforth of all the rest,
Be thou the River,
Which as the daintiest,
Puts them downe ever,
For as my precious one,
O'r thee doth trauell,
She to Pearl Parragon
Turneth thy grauell.

CHORUS
On thy Bancke,
In a Rancke,
Let thy Swanns sing her,

And with their Musicke,
Along let them bring her.

Our mournefull Philomell,
That rarest Tuner,
Henceforth in Aperill
Shall wake the sooner,
And to her shall complaine
From the thicke Cover,
Redoubling every straine
Over and over:
For when my Love too long
Her Chamber keepeth;
As though it suffered wrong,
The Morning weepeth.

CHORUS
On thy Bancke,
In a Rancke,
Let thy Swanes sing her,
And with their Musick,
Along let them bring her.

Oft have I seene the Sunne
To doe her honour.
Fix himselfe at his noone,
To look upon her,
And hath guilt every Grove,
Every Hill neare her,
With his flames from above,
Striuing to cheere her,
And when shee from his sight
Hath her selfe turned,
He as it had beene night,
In Cloudes hath mourned.

CHORUS
On thy Bancke,
In a Rancke,
Let thy Swanns sing her,
And with their Musicke,
Along let them bring her.

The Verdant Meades are seene,
When she doth view them,
In fresh and gallant Greene,
Straight to renewe them,
And every little Grasse
Broad it selfe spreadeth,
Proud that this bonny Lasse
Upon it treadeth:

Nor flower is so sweete
In this large Cincture
But it upon her feete
Leaueth some Tincture.

CHORUS
On thy Bancke,
In a Rancke,
Let thy Swanes sing her,
And with thy Musick,
Along let them bring her.

The Fishes in the Flood,
When she doth Angle,
For the Hooke strive a good
Them to intangle;
And leaping on the Land
From the cleare water,
Their Scales upon the sand,
Lauishly scatter;
Therewith to pave the mould
Whereon she passes,
So her selfe to behold,
As in her glasses.

CHORUS
On thy Bancke,
In a Ranke,
Let thy Swanns sing her,
And with their Musicke,
Along let them bring her.

When shee lookes out by night,
The Starres stand gazing,
Like Commets to our sight
Fearefully blazing,
As wondring at her eyes
With their much brightnesse,
Which to amaze the skies,
Dimming their lightnesse,
The raging Tempests are Calme,
When shee speaketh,
Such most delightsome balme
From her lips breaketh.

CHORUS
On thy Bancke,
In a Ranke,
Let thy Swanns sing her,
And with their Musicke,
Along let them bring her.

In all our Brittany,
Ther's not a fayrer,
Nor can you fitt any:
Should you compare her.
Angels her eye-lids keepe
All harts surprizing,
Which looke whilst she doth sleepe
Like the Sunnes rising:
She alone of her kinde
Knoweth true measure
And her unmatched mind
Is Heavens treasure:

CHORUS
On thy Bancke,
In a Rancke
Let thy Swanes sing her,
And with their Musick,
Along let them bring her.

Fayre Doue and Darwine cleere
Boast yee your beauties,
To Trent your Mistres here
Yet pay your duties,
My Love was higher borne
Tow'rds the full Fountaines,
Yet she doth Moorland scorne,
And the Peake Mountaines;
Nor would she none should dreame,
Where she abideth,
Humble as is the streame,
Which by her slydeth,

CHORUS
On thy Bancke,
In a Rancke,
Let thy Swannes sing her,
And with their Musicke,
Along let them bring her.

Yet my poore Rusticke Muse,
Nothing can move her,
Nor the means I can use,
Though her true Lover:
Many a long Winters night,
Have I wak'd for her,
Yet this my piteous plight,
Nothing can stirre her.
All thy Sands silver Trent
Downe to the Humber,

The sighes I have spent
Never can number.

CHORUS
On thy Banke
In a Ranke,
Let thy Swans sing her
And with their Musicke
Along let them bring her.

Taken with this suddaine Song,
Least for mirth when he doth look
His sad heart more deeply stong,
Then the former care he tooke.
At their laughter and amaz'd,
For a while he sat aghast
But a little having gaz'd,
Thus he them bespake at last.
Is this time for mirth (quoth he)
To a man with griefe opprest,
Sinfull wretches as you be,
May the sorrowes in my breast,
Light upon you one by one,
And as now you mocke my woe,
When your mirth is turn'd to moane;
May your like then serue you so.
When one Swaine among the rest
Thus him merrily bespake,
Get thee up thou arrant beast
Fits this season love to make?
Take thy Sheephooke in thy hand,
Clap thy Curre and set him on,
For our fields 'tis time to stand,
Or they quickly will be gon.
Rougish Swinheards that repine
At our Flocks, like beastly Clownes,
Sweare that they will bring their Swine,
And will wroote up all our Downes:
They their Holly whips have brac'd,
And tough Hazell goades have gott;
Soundly they your sides will baste,
If their courage faile them not.
Of their purpose if they speed,
Then your Bagpypes you may burne,
It is neither Droane nor Reed
Shepheard, that will serue your turne:
Angry OLCON sets them on,
And against us part doth take
Ever since he was out-gone,
Offring Rymes with us to make.
Yet if so our Sheepe-hookes hold,

Dearely shall our Downes be bought,
For it never shall be told,
We our Sheep-walkes sold for naught.
And we here have got us Dogges,
Best of all the Westerne breed,
Which though Whelps shall lug their Hogges,
Till they make their eares to bleed:
Therefore Shepheard come away.
When as DORILUS arose,
Whistles Cut-tayle from his play,
And along with them he goes.

COMMENDATORY & OTHER VERSES

From England's Helicon (1600)

Rowlands Madrigall

Faire Love rest thee heere,
Never yet was morne so cleere,
Sweete be not unkinde,
Let me thy favour finde,
Or else for love I die.

Harke this pretty bubling spring,
How it makes the Meadowes ring,
Love now stand my friend,
Heere let all sorrow end,
And I will honour thee.

See where little Cupid lyes,
Looking babies in her eyes.
Cupid helpe me now,
Lend to me thy bowe,
To wound her that wounded me.

Heere is none to see or tell,
All our flocks are feeding by,
This Banke with Roses spred,
Oh it is a dainty bed,
Fit for my Love and me.

Harke the birds in yonder Groaue,
How they chaunt unto my Love,
Love be kind to me,
As I have beene to thee,
For thou hast wonne my hart.

Calme windes blow you faire,

Rock her thou gentle ayre,
O the morne is noone,
The euening comes too soone,
To part my Love and me.

The Roses and thy lips doo meete,
Oh that life were halfe so sweete,
Who would respect his breath,
That might die such a death,
Oh that life thus might die.

All the bushes that be neere,
With sweet Nightingales beset,
Hush sweete and be still,
Let them sing their fill,
There's none our joyes to let.

Sunne why doo'st thou goe so fast?
Oh why doo'st thou make such hast?
It is too early yet,
So soone from joyes to flit
Why art thou so unkind?

See my little Lambkins runne,
Looke on them till I have done,
Hast not on the night,
To rob me of her light,
That live but by her eyes.

Alas, sweete Love, we must depart,
Harke, my dogge begins to barke,
Some bodie's comming neere,
They shall not find us heere,
For feare of being chid.

Take my Garland and my Glove,
Weare it for my sake my Love,
To morrow on the greene,
Thou shalt be our Sheepheards Queene,
Crowned with Roses gay.

From T. Morley's First Book of Ballets (1595).

Mr. M.D. to the Author.

Such was old Orpheus cunning,
That sencelesse things drew neere him,
And heards of beasts to heare him,
The stock, the stone, the Oxe, the Asse came running,

Morley! but this enchaunting
To thee, to be the Musick-God is wanting.
And yet thou needst not feare him;
Draw thou the Shepherds still and Bonny lasses,
And enuie him not stocks, stones, Oxen, Asses.

Prefixed to Christopher Middleton's Legend of Humphrey Duke of Gloucester (1600).

To His friend, Master Chr. M. His Booke.

Like as a man, on some aduenture bound
His honest friendes, their kindnes to expresse,
T'incourage him of whome the maine is own'd;
Some venture more, and some aduenture lesse,
That if the voyage (happily) be good:
They his good fortune freely may pertake;
If otherwise it perrish in the flood,
Yet like good friends theirs perish'd for his sake.
On thy returne I put this little forth,
My chaunce with thine indifferently to prove,
Which though (I know) not fitting with thy worth,
Accept it yet since it proceedes from love;
And if thy fortune prosper, I may see
I have some share, though most returne to thee.

Prefixed to John Davies of Hereford; Holy Roode (1609).

To M. John Davies, My Good Friend.

Such men as hold intelligence with Letters,
And in that nice and Narrow way of Verse,
As oft they lend, so oft they must be Debters,
If with the Muses they will have commerce:
Seldome at Stawles, me, this way men rehearse,
To mine Inferiours, not unto my Betters:
He stales his Lines that so doeth them disperse;
I am so free, I love not Golden-fetters.
And many Lines fore Writers, be but Setters
To them which cheate with Papers; which doth pierse,
Our Credits: when we shew our selves Abetters:
To those that wrong our knowledge: we rehearse
Often (my good John; and I love) thy Letters;
Which lend me Credit, as I lend my Verse.

Prefixed to Sir David Murray's Sophonisba &c. (1611).

To My Kinde Friend Da: Murray.

In new attire (and put most neatly on)
Thou Murray mak'st thy passionate Queene apeare,
As when she sat on the Numidian throne,
Deck'd with those Gems that most refulgent were.
So thy stronge muse her maker like repaires,
That from the ruins of her wasted vrne,
Into a body of delicious ayres:
Againe her spirit doth transmigrated turne,
That scortching soile which thy great subiect bore,
Bred those that coldly but exprest her merit,
But breathing now upon our colder shore,
Here shee hath found a noble fiery spirit,
Both there, and here, so fortunate for Fame,
That what she was, she's every where the same.

Among the Panegyrical Verses before Coryat's Crudities (1611).

Incipit Michael Drayton.

A briefe Prologue to the verses following.

Deare Tom, thy booke was like to come to light,
Ere I could gaine but one halfe howre to write;
They go before whose wits are at their noones,
And I come after bringing Salt and Spoones.

Many there be that write before thy Booke,
For whom (except here) who could ever looke?
Thrice happy are all wee that had the Grace
To have our names set in this living place.
Most worthy man, with thee it is euen thus,
As men take Dottrels, so hast thou ta'n us.
Which as a man his arme or leg doth set,
So this fond Bird will likewise counterfeit:
Thou art the Fowler, and doest shew us shapes
And we are all thy Zanies, thy true Apes.
I saw this age (from what it was at first)
Swolne, and so bigge, that it was like to burst,
Growne so prodigious, so quite out of fashion,
That who will thriue, must hazard his damnation:
Sweating in panges, sent such a horrid mist,
As to dim heaven: I looked for Antichrist
Or some new set of Diuels to sway hell,
Worser then those, that in the Chaos fell:
Wondring what fruit it to the world would bring,
At length it brought forth this: O most strange thing;

And with sore throwes, for that the greatest head
Ever is hard'st to be delivered.
By thee wise Coryate we are taught to know,
Great, with great men which is the way to grow.
For in a new straine thou com'st finely in,
Making thy selfe like those thou mean'st to winne:
Greatnesse to me seem'd ever full of feare,
Which thou found'st false at thy arriuing there,
Of the Bermudas, the example such,
Where not a ship untill this time durst touch;
Kep't as suppos'd by hels infernall dogs,
Our Fleet found their most honest wyld courteous hogs.
Live vertuous Coryate, and for ever be
Lik'd of such wise men, as are most like thee.

Prefixed to William Browne's Britannia's Pastorals (1613).

To His Friend the Author.

Drive forth thy Flocke, young Pastor, to that Plaine,
Where our old Shepheards wont their flocks to feed;
To those cleare walkes, where many a skilfull Swaine
To'ards the calme eu'ning, tun'd his pleasant Reede,
Those, to the Muses once so sacred, Downes,
As no rude foote might there presume to stand:
(Now made the way of the unworthiest Clownes,
Dig'd and plow'd up with each unhallowed hand)
If possible thou canst, redeeme those places,
Where, by the brim of many a silver Spring,
The learned Maydens, and delightfull Graces
Often have sate to heare our Shepheards sing:
Where on those Pines the neighb'ring Groves among,
(Now vtterly neglected in these dayes)
Our Garlands, Pipes, and Cornamutes were hong
The monuments of our deserued praise.
So may thy Sheepe like, so thy Lambes increase,
And from the Wolfe feede ever safe and free!
So maist thou thriue, among the learned prease,
As thou young Shepheard art belou'd of mee!

Prefixed to Chapman's Translation of Hesiod's Georgics (1618).

To My Worthy Friend Mr. George Chapman, and His Translated Hesiod.

Chapman; We finde by thy past-prized fraught,
What wealth thou dost upon this Land conferre;
Th'olde Grecian Prophets hither that hast brought,

Of their full words the true interpreter:
And by thy trauell, strongly hast exprest
The large dimensions of the English tongue;
Delivering them so well, the first and best,
That to the world in Numbers ever sung.
Thou hast unlock'd the treasury, wherein
All Art, and knowledge have so long been hidden:
Which, till the gracefull Muses did begin
Here to inhabite, was to us forbidden.
In blest Elizivm (in a place most fit)
Under that tree due to the Delphian God,
Musæus, and that Iliad Singer sit,
And neare to them that noble Hesiod,
Smoothing their rugged foreheads; and do smile,
After so many hundred yeares to see
Their Poems read in this farre westerne Ile,
Translated from their ancient Greeke, by thee;
Each his good Genius whispering in his eare,
That with so lucky, and auspicious fate
Did still attend them, whilst they living were,
And gaue their Verses such a lasting date.
Where slightly passing by the Thespian spring,
Many long after did but onely sup;
Nature, then fruitfull, forth these men did bring,
To fetch deep Rowses from Joves plentious cup.
In thy free labours (friend) then rest content,
Feare not Detraction, neither fawne on Praise:
When idle Censure all her force hath spent,
Knowledge can crowne her self with her owne Baies.
Their Lines, that have so many lives outworne,
Cleerely expounded shall base Enuy scorne.

Prefixed to Book II. of Primaleon, &c. Translated by Anthony Munday (1619).

Of the Work and Translation.

If in opinion of judiciall wit,
Primaleons sweet Invention well deserue:
Then he (no lesse) which hath translated it,
Which doth his sense, his forme, his phrase, obserue.
And in true method of his home-borne stile,
(Following the fashion of a French conceate)
Hath brought him heere into this famous Ile,
Where but a stranger, now hath made his seate.
He lives a Prince, and comming in this sort,
Shall to his Countrey of your fame report.

Michael Drayton.

From Annalia Dubrensia (1636).

To My Noble Friend Mr Robert Dover, On His Brave Annual Assemblies Upon Cotswold.

Dover, to doe thee Right, who will not strive,
That dost in these dull yron Times reuiue
The golden Ages glories; which poore Wee
Had not so much as dream't on but for Thee?
As those brave Grecians in their happy dayes,
On Mount Olympus to their Hercules
Ordain'd their games Olimpick, and so nam'd
Of that great Mountaine; for those pastimes fam'd:
Where then their able Youth, Leapt, Wrestled, Ran,
Threw the arm'd Dart; and honour'd was the Man
That was the Victor; In the Circute there
The nimble Rider, and skill'd Chariotere
Stroue for the Garland; In those noble Times
There to their Harpes the Poets sang their Rimes;
That whilst Greece flourisht, and was onely then
Nurse of all Arts, and of all famous men:
Numbring their yeers, still their accounts they made,
Either from this or that Olimpiade.
So Dover, from these Games, by thee begun,
Wee'l reckon Ours, as time away doth run.
Wee'l have thy Statue in some Rocke cut out,
With brave Inscriptions garnished about;
And under written, Loe, this was the man,
DOVER, that first these noble Sports began.
Ladds of the Hills, and Lasses of the Vale,
In many a song, and many a merry Tale
Shall mention Thee; and having leaue to play,
Unto thy name shall make a Holy day.
The Cosswold Shepheards as their flockes they keepe,
To put off lazie drowsinesse and sleepe,
Shall sit to tell, and heare thy Story tould,
That night shall come ere they their flocks can fould.

Michael Drayton.

ENDIMON AND PHŒBE

IDEAS LATMUS

Phœbus erit nostri princeps, et carminis Author.

To the Excellent and Most Accomplisht Ladie: Lucie Countesse of Bedford.

Great Ladie, essence of my cheefest good,
Of the most pure and finest tempred spirit
Adornd with gifts, enobled by the blood,
Which by discent true vertue do'st inherit;
That vertue which no fortune can depriue,
Which most in honor shall excell the other;
Unto thy fame my Muse her selfe shall taske,
Which rain'st upon mee thy sweet golden shower
And but thy selfe, no subiect will I aske,
Upon whose praise my soule shall spend her power.
Sweet Ladie then, grace this poore Muse of mine,
Whose faith, whose zeale, whose life, whose all is thine.

Your Honors humbly
devoted
Michael Drayton

Rowland When First I Read Thy Stately Rymes

In Sheepheards weedes, when yet thou liv'dst unknowne,
Not seene in publique in those former tymes,
But unto Ankor tund'st thy Pype alone
I then beheld thy chaste Ideas fame
Put on the wings of thine immortall stile,
whose rarest vertues, and deserued name
Thy Muse renowns throughout this glorious Ile,
Thy lines, like to the Lawrells pleasant shade,
In after ages shall adorne her Herse,
Nor can her beauties glory fade
Deckt in the collours of thy happy verse.
Thy fiery spirit mounts up to the skye,
And what thou writ'st lives to Eternitye.

E. P.

To Idea

A Midst those shades wherein the Muses sit,
Thus to Idea, my Idea sings,
Support of wisedome, better force of Wit:
Which by desert, desert to honour brings,
Borne to create good thoughts by thy rare woorth,
Whom Nature with her bounteous store doth blesse,
More excellent then Art can set thee forth;
Happy in more, then praises can expresse:
Which by thy selfe shalt make thy selfe continue,
When all worlds glory shall be cleane forgot,
Thus I the least of skilfull Arts retinue:

Write in thy prayse which time shall never blot;

Heaven made thee what thou art, till worlds be done,
Thy fame shall flourish like the rising Sunne.

S. G.

Endimion & Phœbe

Ideas Latmus.

In I-onia whence sprang old Poets fame,
From whom that Sea did first derive her name,
The blessed bed whereon the Muses lay,
Beauty of Greece, the pride of Asia,
Whence Archelaus whom times historifie,
First unto Athens brought Phylosophie.
In this faire Region on a goodly Plaine,
Stretching her bounds unto the bordering Maine,
The Mountaine Latmus over-lookes the Sea,
Smiling to see the Ocean billowes play:
Latmus, where young Endimion usd to keepe
His fairest flock of silver-fleeced sheepe.
To whom Siluanus often would resort,
At barly-breake to see the Satyres sport;
And when rude Pan his Tabret list to sound,
To see the faire Nymphes foote it in a round,
Under the trees which on this Mountaine grew,
As yet the like Arabia never knew:
For all the pleasures Nature could devise,
Within this plot she did imparadize;
And great Diana of her speciall grace,
With Vestall rytes had hallowed all the place:
Upon this Mount there stood a stately Grove,
Whose reaching armes, to clip the Welkin strove,
Of tufted Cedars, and the branching Pine,
Whose bushy tops themselves doe so intwine,
As seem'd when Nature first this work begun,
Shee then conspir'd against the piercing Sun;
Under whose covert (thus divinely made)
Phœbus greene Laurell florisht in the shade:
Faire Venus Mirtile, Mars his warlike Fyrre,
Mineruas Olive, and the weeping Myrhe,
The patient Palme, which thriues in spite of hate,
The Popler, to Alcides consecrate;
Which Nature in such order had disposed,
And there withall those goodly walkes inclosed,
As serv'd for hangings and rich Tapestry,
To beautifie this stately Gallery:

Imbraudring these in dutious trailes along,
The clustred Grapes, the golden Citrons hung,
More glorious then the precious fruite were these,
Kept by the Dragon in Hesperides;
Or gorgious Arras in rich colours wrought,
With silk from Affrick, or from Indie brought:
Out of this soyle sweet bubbling Fountains crept,
As though for joy the sencelesse stones had wept;
With straying channels dauncing sundry wayes,
With often turnes, like to a curious Maze:
Which breaking forth, the tender grasse bedewed
Whose silver sand with orient Pearle was strewed,
Shadowed with Roses and sweet Eglantine,
Dipping theyr sprayes into this christalline:
From which the byrds the purple berries pruned,
And to theyr loves their small recorders tuned.
The Nightingale, woods Herauld of the Spring,
The whistling Woosell, Mauis carroling,
Tuning theyr trebbles to the waters fall,
Which made the musicque more angelicall:
Whilst gentle Zephyre murmuring among,
Kept tyme, and bare the burthen to the song.
About whose brims, refresht with dainty showers,
Grew Amaranthus, and sweet Gilliflowers,
The Marigold, Phœbus beloved frend,
The Moly, which from sorcery doth defend:
Violet, Carnation, Balme, and Cassia,
Ideas Primrose, coronet of May.
Above the Grove a gentle faire ascent,
Which by degrees of Milk-white Marble went:
Upon the top, a Paradise was found,
With which, Nature this miracle had crownd;
Empald with Rocks of rarest precious stone,
Which like the flames of Aetna brightly shone;
And seru'd as Lanthornes furnished with light,
To guide the wandring passengers by night:
For which fayre Phœbe sliding from her Sphere,
Used oft times to come and sport her there.
And from the Azure starry-painted Sky,
Embalmd the bancks with precious lunary:
That now her Menatus she quite forsooke,
And unto Latmus wholy her betooke,
And in this place her pleasure us'd to take,
And all was for her sweet Endimions sake:
Endimion, the lovely Shepheards boy,
Endimion, great Phœbes onely joy,
Endimion, in whose pure-shining eyes,
The naked Faries daunst the heydegies.
The shag-haird Satyrs Mountain-climing race,
Have been made tame by gazing in his face.
For this boyes love, the water Nymphs have wept

Stealing oft times to kisse him whilst he slept:
And tasting once the Nectar of his breath,
Surfet with sweet, and languish unto death;
And loue oft-times bent to lasciuious sport,
And comming where Endimion did resort,
Hath courted him, inflamed with desire,
Thinking some Nymph was cloth'd in boyes attire.
Beholding him in crossing or'e the Plaines,
Imagined, Apollo from above
Put on this shape, to win some Maidens love.
This Shepheard, Phœbe ever did behold,
Whose love already had her thoughts controld;
From Latmus top (her stately throne) shee rose,
And to Endimion downe beneath shee goes.
Her Brothers beames now had shee layd aside,
her horned cressent, and her full-fac'd pride:
For had shee come adorned with her light,
No mortall eye could have endur'd the sight;
But like a Nymph, crown'd with a flowrie twine,
And not like Phœbe, as herself divine.
An Azur'd Mantle purfled with a vaile,
Which in the Ayre puft like a swelling saile,
Embosted Rayne-bowes did appeare in silk,
With wauie streames as white as mornings Milk:
Which ever as the gentle Ayre did blow,
Still with the motion seem'd to ebb and flow:
About her neck a chayne twise twenty fold,
Of Rubyes, set in lozenges of gold;
Trust up in trammels, and in curious pleats,
With spheary circles falling on her teats.
A dainty smock of Cipresse, fine and thin,
Or'e cast with curls next to her Lilly skin:
Throgh which the purenes of the same did show
Like Damaske-roses strew'd with flakes of snow.
Discovering all her stomack to the waste,
With branches of sweet circling veynes enchaste.
A Coronet she ware of Mirtle bowes,
Which gaue a shadow to her Iuory browes.
No smother beauty maske did beauty smother
"Great lights dim lesse yet burn not one another,
Nature abhorrs to borrow from the Mart,
"Simples fit beauty, fie on drugs and Art.

Thus came shee where her love Endimion lay,
Who with sweet Carrols sang the night away;
And as it is the Shepheards usuall trade,
Oft on his pype a Roundelay he playd.
As meeke he was as any Lambe might be,
Nor never lyu'd a fayrer youth then he:
His dainty hand, the snow it selfe dyd stayne,
Or her to whom loue showr'd in golden rayne:

From whose sweet palme the liquid Pearle dyd swell,
Pure as the drops of Aganippas Well:
Cleere as the liquor which fayre Hebe spylt;
Hys sheephooke silver, damask'd all with gilt.
The staffe it selfe, of snowie luory,
Studded with Currall, tipt with Ebony;
His tresses, of the Rauens shyning black,
Stragling in curles along his manly back.
The balls which nature in his eyes had set,
Lyke Diamonds inclosing Globes of Iet:
Which sparkled from their milky lids out-right,
Lyke fayre Orions heaven-adorning light.

The stars on which her heavenly eyes were bent,
And fixed still with lovely blandishment,
For whom so oft disguised shee was seene,
As shee Celestiall Phœbe, had not beene:
Her dainty Buskins lac'd unto the knee,
Her pleyted Frock, tuck'd up accordingly:
A nymph-like huntresse, arm'd with bow & dart
About the woods she scoures the long-hu'd Hart.
Se climes the mountains with the light-foot Fauns
And with the Satyrs scuds it or'e the Launes.
In Musicks sweet delight shee shewes her skill,
Quauering the Cithrons nimbly with her quill,
Upon each tree she carues Endimions name
In Gordian knots, with Phœbe to the same:
To kill him Venson now she pitch'd her toyles,
And to this lovely Raunger brings the spoyles;
And thus whilst shee by chaste desire is led
Unto the Downes where he his fayre Flocks fed,
Neere to a Grove she had Endimion spide,
Where he was fishing by a River side
Under a Popler, shadowed from the Sun,
Where merrily to court him she begun:
Sweet boy (qd. she) take what thy hart can wish,
When thou doost angle would I were a fish,
When thou art sporting by the silver Brooks,
Put in thy hand thou need'st no other hooks;
Hard harted boy Endimion looke on mee,
Nothing on earth I hold too deere for thee:
I am a Nimph and not of humaine blood,
Begot by Pan on Isis sacred flood:
When I was borne upon that very day,
Phœbus was seene the Reueller to play:
In Ioves hye house the Gods assembled all,
And Iuno held her sumptuous Festiuall,
Oceanus that hower was dauncing spy'de,
And Tython seene to frolick with his Bride,
The Halcions that season sweetly sang,
And all the shores, with shouting Sea-Nymphes rang,

And on that day, my birth to memorize,
The Shepheards hold a solemne sacrifice:
The chast Diana nusrt mee in her lap,
And I suckt Nectar from her downe-soft pap.
The Well wherein this body bathed first,
Who drinks thereof, shall never after thirst;
The water hath the Lunacie appeased,
And by the vertue, cureth all diseased;
The place wherein my bare feete touch the mold,
Made up in balls, for Pomander is sold.
See, see, these hands have robd the Snow of white,
These dainty fingers, organs of delight;
Behold these lyps, the Load-stones of desire,
Whose words inchant, like Amphyous well-tun'd lyre,
Signing the earth wit heavens own manuel seale.
Goe, play the wanton, I will tend thy flock,
And wait the hours as duly as a clock;
Ile deck thy Ram with bells, and wreathes of Bay,
And gild his hornes upon the sheering day.
And with a garlond crown thee Shepheards king,
And thou shalt lead the gay Gyrles in a ring;
Birds with their wings shall fan thee in the Sun,
And all the fountaynes with pure Wine shall run,
I have a Quier of dainty Turle-doues,
And they shall sit and sweetly sing our loves:
Ile lay thee on the Swans soft downy plume,
And all the Winde shall gently breath perfume,
Ile plat thy locks with many a curious pleate,
And chase thy temples with a sacred heate;
The Muses still shall keepe thee company,
And lull thee with inchaunting harmony;
If not all these, yet let my vertues move thee,
A chaster Nymph Endimion cannot love thee.

But he imagin'd she some Nymph had been,
Because shee was apparreled in greene:
Or happily, some of fayre Floras trayne,
Which oft did use to sport upon the Plaine:
He tels her, he was Phœbes seruant sworne,
And oft in hunting had her Quiver borne,
And that to her verginity he vowed,
Which in no hand by Venus was allowed;
Then unto her a Catalogue he cites
Of Phœbes Statutes, and her hallowed Rites,
And of the grieuous penalty inflicted,
On such as her chast lawes had interdicted:
Now, he requests, that see would stand aside,
Because the fish her shadow had espide;
Then he intreats her that she would be gone,
And at this time to let him be alone;
Then turnes him from her in an angry sort,

And frownes and chafes that shee had spoil'd his sport.
And told her, great Diana came this way.
But for all this, the Nymph would not forbeare,
But now she smoothes his crispy-curled haire,
And when hee (rudely) will'd her to refrayne,
Yet scarcely ended, she begins agayne:
Thy Ewes (quoth she) with Milk shall daily spring,
And to thy profit yeerely Twins shall bring,
And thy fayre flock, (a wonder to behold)
Shall have their fleeces turn'd to burnisht gold;
Thy batefull pasture to thy wanton Thewes,
Shall be refresht with Nectar-dropping dewes,
The Oakes smooth leaues, sirropt with hony fall,
Trickle down drops to quench thy thirst withall:
The cuell Tyger will I tame for thee,
And gently lay his head upon thy knee;
And by my spells, the Wolues iawes will I lock,
And (as good Sheepheards) make them gard thy flock,
Ile mount thee bravely on a Lyons back,
To driue the fomy-tusked Bore to wrack:
The brazen-hoofed yelling Bulls Ile yoke,
And with my hearbs, the scaly Dragon choke.
Thou in great Phœbes Iuery Coche shalt ride,
Which drawne by Eagles, in the ayre shall glide:
Ile stay the time, it shall not steale away,
And twenty Moones as seeming but one day.
Behold (fond boy) this Rozen-weeping Pine,
This mournfull Larix, dropping Turpentine,
This mounting Teda, thus with tempests torne,
With incky teares continually to mourne;
Looke on this tree, which blubbereth Amber gum
which seemes to speak to thee, though it be dumb,
Which being senceles blocks, as thou do'st see,
Weepe at my woes, that thou might'st pitty mee:
O thou art young, and fit for loues profession,
Like wax which warmed quickly takes impression,
Sorrow in time, with floods those eyes shall weare,
Whence pitty now cannot extort a teare.
Fond boy, with words thou might'st be overcome,
"But love surpriz'd the hart, the tongue is dumbe,
But as I can, Ile strive to conquer thee;
Yet teares, & sighes, my weapons needs must bee.
My sighs move trees, rocks melting with my tears,
But thou art blind; and cruell stop'st thine eares:
Looke in this Well, (if beautie men alow)
Though thou be faire, yet I as faire as thou;
I am a Vestall, and a spotless Mayd,
Although by love to thee I am betrayd:
But sith (unkinde) thou doost my love disdayne,
To rocks and hills my selfe I will complaine.

Thus with a sigh, her speeches of she broke,
The whilst her eyes to him in silence spoke;
And from the place this wanton Nymph arose,
And up to Latmos all in hast she goes;
Like to a Nymph on shady Citheron,
The swift Ismænos, or Thirmodoon
Gliding like Thetis, on the fleet waues borne,
Or she which trips upon the eares of Corne;
Like Swallowes when in open ayre they strive,
Or like the Foule which towring Falcons driue.
But whilst the wanton thus pursu'd his sport,
Deceitfull Love had undermin'd the fort,
And by a breach (in spight of all deniance,)
Entred the Fort which lately made defiance:
And with strong siedge had now begirt about
The mayden Skonce which held the souldier out.
"Love wants his eyes, yet shoots he passing right,
His shafts our thoughts, his bowe hee makes our sight.
His deadly piles are tempred by such Art,
As still directs the Arrowe to the hart:
He cannot love, and yet forsooth he will,
He sees her not, and yet he sees her still,
Hee goes unto the place shee stood upon,
And asks the poore soyle whether she was gon;
Fayne would he follow her, yet makes delay,
Fayne would he goe, and yet fayne would he stay,
Hee kist the flowers depressed with her feete,
And swears from her they borrow'd all their sweet.
Faine would he cast aside this troublous thought,
But still like poyson, more and more it wrought,
And to himselfe thus often would he say,
Heere my Love sat, in this place did she play,
Heere in this Fountaine hath my Goddesse been,
And with her presence hath she grac'd this green.

Now black-brow'd Night plac'd in her chaire of Iet,
Sat wrapt in clouds within her Cabinet,
And with her dusky mantle over-spred,
The path the Sunny Palfrayes us'd to tred,
And Cynthia sitting in her Christall chayre,
In all her pompe now rid along her Spheare,
The honnied dewe descended in soft showres,
Drizled in Pearle upon the tender flowers;
And Zephyre husht, and with a whispering gale,
Seemed to harken to the Nightingale,
Which in the thorny brakes with her sweet song,
Unto the silent Night bewrayed her wrong.

Now fast by Latmus neere unto a Grove,
Which by the mount was shadowed from above,
Upon a banck Endimion sat by night,

To whom fayre Phœbe lent her friendly light:
And sith his flocks were layd them down to rest,
Thus gives his sorrowes passage from his brest;
Sweet leaues (qd. he) which with the ayre do tremble,
Oh how your motions do my thoughts resemble,
With that milde breath, by which you onely move,
Whisper my words in silence to my Love:
Conuay my sighes sweet Ciuet-breathing ayre,
In dolefull accents to my heavenly fayre;
You murmuring Springs, like doleful Instruments
Upon your grauell sound my sad laments,
And in your silent bubling as you goe,
Consort your selues like Musick to my woe.
And lifting now his sad and heavy eyes
Up, towards the beauty of the burnisht skies,
Bright Lamps (qd. he) the glorious Welkin bears,
Which clip about the Plannets wandring Sphears,
And in your circled Maze doe ever role,
Daucing about the never moouing Pole:
Sweet Nymph, which in fayre Elice doost shine,
Whom thy surpassing beauty made divine,
Now in the Artick constellation,
Smyle sweet Calisto on Endimion:
And thou brave Perseus in the Northern ayre,
Holding Medusa by the snaky hayre,
Joves showre-begotten Son, whose valure tryed,
In seuenteene glorious lights art stellified;
Which won'st thy love, left as a Monster pray,
And thou the lovely fayre Andromida,
Borne of the famous Etheopian lyne,
Darting those rayes from thy transpiercing eyne,
To thee the bright Cassiopey, with these,
Whose beauty stroue with the Neriedes,
With all the troupe of the celestiall band,
Which on Olimpus in your glory stand;
And you great wandring lights, if from your Sphears
You have regard unto a Sheepeheards teares,
Or as men say, if over earthly things
You onely rule as Potentates and Kings,
Unto my loves euent sweet Stars direct,
Your kindest reuolution and aspect,
And bend your cleere eyes from your Thrones above
Upon Endimion pyning thus in love.

Now, ere the purple dauning yet did spring,
The joyfull Lark began to stretch her wing,
And now the Cock the mornings Trumpeter,
Playd hunts-up for the day starre to appeare,
Downe slydeth Phœbe from her Christall chayre,
Sdayning to lend her light unto the ayre,
But unto Latmus all in haste is gon,

Longing to see her sweet Endimion;
At whose departure all the Plannets gazed,
As at some seld-seene accident amazed,
Till reasoning of the same, they fell at ods,
So that a question grew amongst the Gods,
Whether without a generall consent
She might depart their sacred Parliament?
But what they could doe was but all in vaine,
Of liberty they could her not restraine:
For of the heaven sith she the lowest was,
Unto the earth she might the easiest passe;
Sith onely by her moysty influence,
Of earthly things she hath prehemimence,
And under her, mans mutable estate,
As with her changes doth participate;
And from the working of her waning source,
Th'uncertaine waters held a certaine course,
Throughout her kingdome she might walk at large
Wherof as Empresse she had care and charge,
And as the Sunne unto the Day gives light,
So is she onely Mistris of the Night;
Which whilst shee in her oblique course dooth guide,
The glittering stars apeare in all their pride,
Which to her light their friendly Lamps do lend,
And on her trayne as Hand-maydes doe atend,
And thirteene times she through her Sphere doth run,
Ere Phœbus fall his yearly course have don:
And unto her of wanton is assign'd,
Predominance of body and of mind,
That as of Plannets shee most variable,
So of all creatures they most mutable;
But her sweet Latmus which she lou'd so much,
No sooner once her dainty foote doth touch,
But that the Mountaine with her brightnes shone
And gaue a light to all the Horizon:
Euen as the Sun which darknes long did shroud,
Breakes suddainly from underneath a clowd,
So that the Nimphs which on her still attended,
Knew certainly great Phœbe was discended;
And all aproched to this sacred hill,
There to awayt their soveraigne Goddesse will,
And now the little Birds whom Nature taught,
To honour great Diana as they ought,
Because she is the Goddesse of the woods,
And sole preseruer of their hallowed floods,
Set to their consort in their lower springs,
That with the Musicke all the mountaine rings;
So that it seemd the Birds of every Grove
Which should excell and passe each other stroue,
That in the higher woods and hollow grounds,
The murmuring Eccho every where resounds,

The trembling brooks their slyding courses stayd,
The whilst the waues one with another playd,
And all the flocks in this rejoycing mood,
As though inchaunted do forbeare their food:
The heards of Deare downe from the mountains flew,
As loth to come within Dianas view,
Whose piercing arrowes from her Iuory bowe,
Had often taught her powerfull hand to knowe;
And now from Latmus looking towards the plains
Casting her eyes upon the Sheepheards swaines,
Perceiu'd her deare Endimions flock were stray'd
And he himselfe upon the ground was layd;
Who late recald from melancholy deepe,
The chaunting Birds had lulled now asleepe:
For why the Musick in this humble kinde,
As it first found, so doth it leaue the minde;
And melancholy from the Spleene begun,
By passion moou'd, into the veynes doth run;
Which when this humor as a swelling Flood
By vigor is infused in the blood;
The vitall spirits doth mightely apall;
And weakeneth so the parts organicall,
And when the sences are disturbed and tierd,
With what the hart incessantly desierd,
Like Travellers with labor long opprest,
Finding release, eft-soones they fall to rest.

And comming now to her Endimion,
Whom heauy sleepe had lately ceas'd upon,
Kneeling her downe, him in her armes she clips,
And with sweet kisses sealeth up his lips,
Whilst from his eyes, teares streaming downe in showers
Fell on his cheekes like dew upon the flowers,
In globy circles like pure drops of Milk,
Sprinckled on Roses, or fine crimson silk:
Touching his brow, this is the seate (quoth she)
Where Beauty sits in all her Maiestie,
She calls his eye-lids those pure Christall covers
Which rare perfume and precious incense holds,
Shee calls his soft smooth Allablaster skin,
The Lawne which Angels are attyred in,
Sweet face (qd. she) but wanting words I spare thee
Except to heaven alone I should compare thee:
And whilst her words she wasteth thus in vayne,
Sporting herselfe the tyme to entertayne,
The frolick Nymphes with Musicks sacred sound,
Entred the Meddowes dauncing in a round:
And unto Phœbe straight their course direct,
Which now their joyfull comming did expect,
Before whose sweet Balme body doth imbay.
And on the Laurels growing there along,

Their wreathed garlonds all about they hung:
And all the ground within the compasse load,
With sweetest flowers, wheron they lightly troad.
And kneeling softly, kisse him all arew;
Then in brave galiards they them selves aduaunce,
And in the Tryas Bacchus stately daunce;
Then following on fayre Floras gilded trayne,
Into the Griues they thus depart agayne,
And now to shew her powerfull deitie,
Her sweet Endimion more to beautifie,
Into his soule the Goddesse doth infuse,
The fiery nature of a heavenly Muse,
Which in the spirit labouring by the mind
Pertaketh of celestiall things by kind:
For why the soule and grosse corruption,
Of heavenly secrets incomprehensible,
Of which the dull flesh is not sensible.
And by one onely powerfull faculty,
Yet governeth a multiplicity,
Being essentiall, uniforme in all,
Not to be sever'd nor diuiduall,
But in her function holdeth her estate,
By powers divine in her ingenerate,
And holy inspiration conceaueth
What heaven to her by divination breatheth;
But they no sooner to the shades were gone,
Leauing their Goddesse by Endimion;
But by the hand the lovely boy shee takes,
And from his sweet sleepe softly him awakes,
Who being struck into a sodayne feare,
Beholding thus his glorious Goddesse there,
His hart transpirced with this sodayne glance,
became as one late come into a trance:
Wiping his eyes not yet of perfect sight,
Scarcely awak'd amazed at the light,
His cheekes now pale then lovely blushing red,
Which oft increasd, and quickly vanished,
And, as on him her fixed eyes were bent,
So to and fro his colour came and went;
Like to a Christall neere the fire set,
Against the brightnes rightly opposet,
Now doth reteyne the colour of the fame,
And lightly moved againe, reflects the same;
For our affection quickned by her heate,
Allayd and strengthned by a strong conceit,
The minde disturbed foorth-with doth convart,
To an internall passion of the hart,
By motion of that sodaine joy or feare,
Which we receiue either by the aye or eare,
For by retraction of the spirit and blood,
From those exterior parts where first they stood,

Into the center of the body sent,
Returnes againe more strong and vehement:
And in the like extreamitie made cold,
About the same, themselves doe closely hold,
And though the cause be like in this respect,
Works by this meanes a contrary effect.

Thus whilst this passion hotely held his course,
Ebbing and flowing from his springing source,
With the strong fit of this sweet Fever moved,
At sight of her which he intirely loved,
Not knowing yet great Phœbe this should be,
His soveraigne Goddesse, Queene of Chastitie,
Now like a man whom Love had learned Art,
Resolu'd at once his secrets to impart:
But first repeats the torments he had past,
The woes indur'd since tyme he saw her last,
Now he reports he noted whilst she spake,
The bustling windes their murmure often brake,
And being silent, seemd to pause and stay,
To listen to her what she ment to say:
Be kind (quoth he) sweet Nymph unto thy lover,
My soules sole essence, and my sences mover,
Life of my life, pure Image of my hart,
Impressure of Conceit, Inuention, Art,
My vitall spirit, receues his spirit from thee,
Thou art all which ruleth all in me,
Thou art the sap, and life whereby I live,
Which powerfull vigor doost receiue and give;
Thou nourishest the flame wherein I burne,
The North wherto my harts true tuch doth turne.
Pitty my poore flock, see their wofull plight,
Theyr Maister perisht living from thy sight,
Theyr fleeces rent, my tresses all forlorne,
I pyne, whilst they theyr pasture have forborne;
Behold (quoth he) this little flower belowe,
Which heere within this Fountayne brim dooth grow;
With that, a solemne tale begins to tell
Of this fayre flower, and of this holy Well,
A goodly legend, many Winters old,
Learn'd by the Sheepheards sitting by their folde,
How once this Fountayne was a youthfull swaine,
A frolick boy and kept upon the playne,
Unfortunate it hapt to him (quoth he)
To love a fayre Nymph as I nowe love thee,
To her his love and sorrow he imparts,
Which might dissolue a rock of flinty harts;
To her he sues, to her he makes his mone,
But she more deafe and hard then steele or stone;
And thus one day with griefe of mind opprest,
As in this place he layd him downe to rest,

The Gods at length uppon his sorrowes looke,
Transforming him into this pirrling Brooke,
Whose murmuring bubles softly as they creepe,
Falling in drops, the Channell seems to weepe,
But shee thus careles of his misery,
Still spends her dayes in mirth and iollity;
And comming one day to the River side,
Laughing for joy when she the same espyde,
This wanton Nymph in that unhappy hower,
Was heere transformd into this purple flower,
Which towards the water turnes it selfe agayne,
To pitty him by her unkindnes slayne.

She, as it seemd, who all this time attended,
Longing to heare that once his tale were ended,
Now like a iealous woman she repeats,
Mens subtilties, and naturall deceyts;
And by example strives to verifie,
Their ficklenes and vaine inconstancie:
Their hard obdurate harts, and wilfull blindnes,
Telling a storie wholy of unkindnes;
But he, who well perceiued her intent,
And to remove her from this argument,
Now by the sacred Fount he vowes and sweares,
By Lovers sighes, and by her halowed teares,
By holy Latmus now he takes his oath,
That all he spake was in good fayth and troth;
And for no frayle uncertayne doubt should move her,
Vowes secrecie, the crown of a true Lover.

She hearing this, thought time that she reueald,
That kind affection which she long conceald,
Determineth to make her true Love known,
Which shee had borne unto Endimion;
I am no Huntresse, nor no Nymph (quoth she)
As thou perhaps imagin'st me to be,
I am great Phœbe, Latmus sacred Queene,
Who from the skies have hether past unseene,
And by thy chast love hether was I led,
Where full three yeares thy fayre flock have I fed,
Upon these Mountaines and these firtile plaines,
And crownd thee King of all the Sheepheards swaines:
nor never lust my chast thoughts once could move
But sith thou thus hast offerd at my Shrine,
And of the Gods hast held me most divine,
Mine Altars thou with sacrifice hast stord,
And in my Temples hast my name ador'd,
And of all other, most hast honor'd mee,
Great Phœbes glory thou alone shalt see.

Thys spake, she putteth on her brave attire,

As being burnisht in her Brothers fire,
Purer then that Celestiall shining flame
Wherein great loue vnto his Lemmon came,
Which quickly had his pale cheekes over-spred,
And tincted with a lovely blushing red.
Which whilst her Brother Titan for a space,
Withdrew himselfe, to give his sister place,
Shee now is darkned to all creatures eyes,
Whilst in the shadow of the earth she lyes,
For that the earth of nature cold and dry,
A very Chaos of obscurity,
Whose Globe exceeds her compasse by degrees,
Fixd upon her Superficies;
When in his shadow she doth hap to fall,
Dooth cause her darknes to be generall.

Thus whilst he layd his head upon her lap,
She in a fiery Mantle doth him wrap,
And carries him up from this lumpish mould,
Into the skyes, whereas he might behold,
The earth in perfect roundnes of a ball
Exceeding globes most artificiall:
Which in a fixed poynt Nature disposed,
And with the sundry Elements inclosed,
Which as the Center permanent dooth stay,
When as the skies in their diurnal sway,
Strongly maintaine the ever-turning course,
Forced alone by their first moover sourse,
Where he beholds the ayery Regions,
Whereas the clouds and strange impressions,
Maintaynd by coldnes often doe appeare,
And by the highest Region of the ayre,
Unto the cleerest Element of fire,
Which to her silver foot-stoole doth aspire,
Then dooth she mount him up into her Sphere,
Imparting heavenly secrets to him there,
Where lightned by her shining beames hee sees,
The powerfull Plannets, all in their degrees,
Their sundry reuolutions in the skies,
And by their working how they simpathize;
All in theyr circles severally prefixt,
And in due distance each with other mixt:
The mantions which they hold in their estate,
Of which by nature they participate;
And how those signes their severall places take,
Within the compasse of the Zodiacke:
And in their severall triplicities consent,
Unto the nature of an Element,
To which the Plannets do themselves disperce,
Having the guidance of this uniuers,
And do from thence extend their severall powers,

Unto this little fleshy world of ours:
Wherin her Makers workmanship is found,
As in contriuing of this mighty round,
In such strange maner and such fashion wrought,
As doth exceede mans dull and feeble thought,
Guiding us still by their directions;
And that our fleshly frayle complections,
Of elementall natures grounded bee,
With which our dispositions most agree,
Some of the fire and ayre participate,
And some of watry and of earthy state,
As hote and moyst, with chilly cold and dry,
And unto these the other contrary;
And by their influence powerfull on the earth,
Predominant in mans fraile mortall bearth,
And that our lives effects and fortunes are,
As is that happy or unlucky Starre,
Which reigning in our frayle natuitie,
Seales up the secrets of our destinie,
With frendly Plannets in coniunction set,
Or els with other merely opposet:
And now to him her greatest power she lent,
To lift him to the starry Firmament,
Where he beheld that milk stayned place,
By which the Twynns & heavenly Archers trace,
The dogge which doth the furious Lyon beate,
Whose flaming breath increaseth Titans heate,
The teare-distilling mournfull Pliades,
Which on the earth the stormes & tempests raise,
And all the course the constellations run,
When in coniunction with the Moone or Sun,
When towards the fixed Articke they arise,
When towards the Antarticke, falling from our eyes;
And having impt the wings of his desire,
And kindled him, with this cœlestiall fire,
She sets him downe, and vanishing his sight,
Leaues him inwrapped in this true delight:
Now wheresoever he his fayre flock fed,
The Muses still Endimion followed;
His sheepe as white as Swans or driuen snow,
Which beautified the soyle with such a show,
As where hee folded in the darkest Night,
There never needed any other light;
If that he hungred and desired meate,
The Bees would bring him Honny for to eate,
Yet from his lyps would not depart away,
Tyll they were loden with Ambrosia;
And if he thirsted, often there was seene
A bubling Fountaine spring out of the greene,
With Christall liquor fild unto the brim,
Which did present her liquid store to him.

If hee would hunt, the fayre Nymphs at his will,
With Bowes & Quiuers, would attend him still:
And what-soever he desierd to have,
That he obtain'd if hee the same would crave.

And now at length, the joyful tyme drew on,
She meant to honor her Endimion,
And glorifie him on that stately Mount
Whereof the Goddesse made so great account.
Shee sends Joves winged Herauld to the woods,
The neighbour Fountains, & the bordering floods,
Charging the Nymphes which did inhabit there,
upon a day appoynted to appeare,
And to attend her sacred Maiestie
In all theyr pompe and great solemnity.
Having obtaynd great Phœbus free consent,
To further her divine and chast intent,
Which thus imposed as a thing of waight,
In stately troupes appeare before her straight,
The Faunes and Satyres from the tufted Brakes,
Theyr brisly armes wreath'd al about with snakes;
Their sturdy loynes with ropes of Iuie bound,
Theyr horned heads with Woodbine Chaplets crownd,
With Cipresse lauelens, and about their thyes,
The flaggy hayre disorder'd loosely flyes:
Th'Oriades like to the Spartan Mayd,
In Murrie-scyndall gorgiously arrayde:
With gallant greene hayre with silken fillets lac'd,
Woue with flowers in sweet lasciuious wreathes,
Moouing like feather as the light ayre breathes,
With crownes of Mirtle, glorious to behold,
whose leaues are painted with pure drops of gold:
With traines of fine Bisse checker'd all with frets
Of dainty Pincks and precious Violets,
In branched Buskins of fine Cordiwin,
With spangled garters cowne unto the shin,
Fring'd with fine silke, of many a sundry kind,
Which lyke to pennons waued with the wind.
The Hamadriads from their shady Bowers,
Deckt up in Garlonds of the rarest flowers,
Upon the backs of milke-white Bulls were set,
With horne and hoofe as black as any Iet,
Whose collers were great massy golden rings,
Led by their swaynes in twisted silken strings;
Then did the lovely Driades appeare,
On dapled Staggs, which bravely mounted were,
Whose veluet palmes with nosegaies rarely dight,
To all the rest bred wonderfull delight;
And in this sort accompaned with these,
In tryumph rid the warty Niades,
Upon Sea-horses, trapt with shining finns,

Arm'd with their male impenitrable skinns,
Whose scaly crests like Raine-bowes bended hye;
Seeme to controule proud Iris in the sky;
Upon a Charriot was Endimion layd,
In snowy Tissue gorgiously arayd,
Of presious Iuory covered or'e with Lawne,
Which by foure stately Unicornes was drawne,
Of ropes of Orient pearle their traces were,
Pure as the path which dooth in heaven appeare,
With rarest flowers inchaste and over-spred,
Which seru'd as Curtaynes to this glorious bed,
Whose seate of Christal in the Sun-beames shone,
Like thunder-breathing Joves celestiall Throne,
Upon his head a Coronet instald,
Of one intire and mighty Emerald,
With richest Bracelets on his lilly wrists,
Of Hellitropium, linckt with golden twists;
A beuy of fayre Swans, which flying over,
With their large wings him from the Sun do cover,
And easily wafting as he went along,
Doe lull him still with their inchaunting song,
Whilst all the Nimphes on solemne Instruments,
Sound daintie Musick to their sweet laments.

And now great Phœbe in her tryumph came,
With all the titles of her glorious name,
Diana, Delia, Lana, Cynthia,
Virago, Hecate, and Elythia,
Prothiria, Dictinna, Proserpine,
Latona, and Lucina, most divine;
And in her pompe began now to approch,
Mounted aloft upon her Christall Coach,
Drawn or'e the playnes by foure pure milk-white Hinds,
Whose nimble feete seem'd winged with the winds,
Her rarest beauty being now begun,
But newly borrowed from the golden Sun,
Her lovely cressant with a decent space,
By due proportion beautified her face,
Till having fully fild her circled side,
Her glorious fulnes now appeard in pride;
which long her changing brow could not retaine,
But fully waxt, began againe to wane;
Upon her brow (like meteors in the ayre)
Twenty & eyght great gorgious lamps shee bare;
Some, as the Welkin, shining passing bright,
Some not so sumptouous, others lesser light,
Some burne; some other, let theyr faire lights fall,
Composd in order Geometricall;
And to adorne her with a greater grace,
And ad more beauty to her lovely face,
Her richest Globe shee gloriously displayes,

Now that the Sun had hid his golden rayes:
Least that his radiencie should her suppresse,
And so might make her beauty seeme the lesse:
Her stately trayne layd out in azur'd bars,
Poudred all thick with troupes of silver stars:
Her ayrie vesture yet so rare and strange,
As every howre the colour seem'd to change,
Yet still the former beauty doth retaine,
And ever came unto the same againe.
Then fayre Astrea, of the Titans line,
Whom equity and iustice made divine,
Was seated heer upon the silver beame,
And with the raines guides on thos goodly teame,
To whom the Charites led on the way,
Aglaia, Thalia, and Euphrozine,
with princely crownes they in the triumph came,
Imbellished with Phœbes glorious name:
These forth before the mighty Goddesse went,
As Princes Heraulds in a Parliament.
And in their true consorted symphony,
Record sweet songs of Phœbes chastity;
Then followed on the Muses, sacred nyne,
With the first number equally divine,
In Virgins white, whose lovely mayden browes,
Were crowned with tryumphant Lawrell bowes;
And on their garments paynted out in glory,
Their offices and functions in a story,
Imblazoning the furie and conceite
Which on their sacred company awaite;

For none but these were suffered to aproch,
Or once come neere to this celestiall Coach,
But these two of the numbers, nine and three,
Which being od include an unity,
Into which number all things fitly fall,
And therefore named Theologicall:
And first composing of this number nine,
Which of all numbers is the most divine,
From orders of the Angels dooth arise,
Which be contayned in three Hirarchies,
And each of these three Hirarchies in three,
The perfect forme of true triplicity;
And of the Hirarchies I spake of erst,
The glorious Epiphania is the first,
In which the hie celestiall orders been,
Of Thrones, Cirrup, and the Ciraphin;
The second holds the mighty Principates,
The Dominations and the Potestates,
The Ephionia, the third Irarchie,
Which Vertues Angels and Archangels be;
And thus by threes we aptly do define,

And do compose this sacred number nyne,
Yet each of these nyne orders grounded be,
Upon some one particularity,
Then as a Poet I might so infer,
An other order when I spake of her.
From these the Muses onely are derived,
Which of the Angels were in nyne contriued;
These heaven-inspired Babes of memorie,
Which by a like attracting Sympathy,
Apollos Prophets in theyr furies wrought,
And in theyr spirit inchaunting numbers taught,
To teach such as at Poesie repine,
That it is onely heavenly and divine,
And manifest her intellectuall parts,
Sucking the purest of the purest Arts;
And unto these as by a sweet consent,
The Sphery circles are equiualent,
From the first Moover, and the starry heaven,
To glorious Phœbe lowest of the seauen,
Which loue in tunefull Diapazons fram'd,
Of heavenly Musick of the Muses nam'd,
To which the soule in her divinitie,
By her Creator made of harmony,
Whilst she in frayle and mortall flesh dooth live,
To her nyne sundry offices doe give,
Which like the orders of the Angels be,
Prefiguring this by the number nyne,
The soule, like to the Angels is divine:
And from these nines those Conquerers renowned,
Which with the wreaths of triumph oft were crowned.
Which by their vertues gain'd the worthies name
First had this number added to their fame,
Not that the worthiest men were onely nine,
But that the number of it selfe divine,
And as a perfect patterne of the rest,
Which by this holy number are exprest;
Nor Chivalrie this title onely gaynd;
But might as well by wisedome be obtaynd,
Nor in this number men alone included,
But unto women well might be aluded,
Could wit, could worlds, coulde times, could ages find,
This number of Elizas heavenly kind;
And those rare men which learning highly prized
By whom the Constellations were devised,
And by their fauours learning highly graced,
For Orpheus harpe nine starres in heaven placed:
This sacred number to declare thereby,
Her sweet consent and solid harmony,
And mans heroique voyce, which doth impart,
The thought conceued in the inward hart,
Her sweetnes on nine Instruments doth ground,

Else doth she fayle in true and perfect sound.
Now of this three in order to dispose,
Whose trynarie doth iustly nyne compose.
First in the forme of this triplicitie
Is shadowed that mighty Trinitie,
Which still in stedfast unity remayne,
And yet of three one Godhead doe containe;
From this eternall living deitie,
As by a heaven-inspired prophecy,
Divinest Poets first derived these,
The fayrest Graces love-borne Charites;
And in this number Musick first began,
The Lydian, Dorian, and the Phrygian,
Which rauishing in their soule-pleasing vaine,
They made up seauen in a higher strayne;
And all those signes which Phœbus doth ascend,
Before he bring his yearely course to end,
Their several natures mutually agree,
And doe concurre in thys triplicitie;
And those interior sences with the rest,
Which properly pertaine to man and Beast,
Nature herselfe in working so devised,
That in the number they should be comprized.

But to my tale I must returne againe,
Phœbe to Latmus thus conuayde her swayne,
Under a bushie Lawrels pleasing shade,
Amongst whose boughs the Birds sweet Musick made,
Whose fragrant branch-imbosted Cannapy,
Was never pierst with Phœbus burning eye;
Yet never could thys Paradise want light,
Elumin'd still with Phœbes glorious sight:
She layd Endimion on a grassy bed,
With sommers Arras ritchly over-spred,
Where from her sacred Mantion next above,
She might descend and sport her with her love,
Which thirty yeeres the Sheepheards safely kept,
Who in her bosom soft and soundly slept;
Yet as a dreame he thought the tyme not long,
Remayning ever beautifull and yong,
And what in vision there to him be fell,
My weary Muse some other time shall tell.

Deare Collin, let my Muse excused be,
Which rudely thus presumes to sing by thee,
Although her straines be harsh untun'd & ill,
Nor can attayne to thy divinest skill.

And thou the sweet Museus of these times,
Pardon my rugged and unfiled rymes,
Whose scarce invention is too meane and base,

When Delias glorious Muse dooth come in place.

And thou my Goldey which in Sommer dayes,
Hast feasted us with merry roundelayes,
And when my Muse scarce able was to flye,
Didst imp her wings with thy sweete Poesie.

And you the heyres of ever-living fame,
The worthy titles of a Poets name,
Whose skill and rarest excellence is such,
As spitefull Envy never yet durst tuch,
To your protection I this Poem send,
Which from proud Momus may my lines defend,

And if sweet mayd thou deign'st to read this story,
Wherein thine eyes may view thy vertues glory,
Thou purest spark of Vesta's kindled fire,
Sweet Nymph of Ankor, crowne of my desire,
The plot which for their pleasure heaven devis'd,
Where all the Muses be imparadis'd,
Where thou doost live, there let all graces be,
Which want theyr grace if onely wanting thee,
Let stormy winter never touch the Clyme,
But let it florish as in Aprils prime,
Let sullen night, that soyle nere over-cloud,
But in thy presence let the earth be proud,
If ever Nature of her worke might boast,
Of thy perfection she may glory most,
To whom fayre Phœbe hath her bow resign'd,
Whose excellence doth lyue in thee refin'd,
And that thy praise Time never should impayre,
Hath made my hart thy never mouing Spheare.
Then if my Muse give life unto thy fame,
Thy vertues be the causers of the same.
And from thy Toombe some Oracle shall rise,
To whom all pens shall yearely sacrifice.

FINIS.

Michael Drayton – A Short Biography by Cyril Brett

Michael Drayton was born in 1563, at Hartshill, near Atherstone, in Warwickshire.

He became a page to Sir Henry Goodere, at Polesworth Hall: his own words give the best picture of his early years here. His education would seem to have been good, but ordinary; and it is very doubtful if he ever went to a university. Besides the authors mentioned in the Epistle to Henry Reynolds, he was certainly familiar with Ovid and Horace, and possibly with Catullus: while there seems no reason to doubt that he read Greek, though it is quite true that his references to Greek authors do not prove any first-hand acquaintance. He understood French, and read Rabelais and the French sonneteers, and he seems to have been acquainted with Italian. His knowledge of English literature was wide, and his judgement good: but his chief bent lay towards the history, legendary and otherwise, of his native country, and his vast stores of learning on this subject bore fruit in the Poly-Olbion.

While still at Polesworth, Drayton fell in love with his patron's younger daughter, Anne; and, though she married, in 1596, Sir Henry Raynsford of Clifford, Drayton continued his devotion to her for many years, and also became an intimate friend of her husband's, writing a sincere elegy on his death.

About February, 1591, Drayton paid a visit to London, and published his first work, the Harmony of the Church, a series of paraphrases from the Old Testament, in fourteen-syllabled verse of no particular vigour or grace. This book was immediately suppressed by order of Archbishop Whitgift, possibly because it was supposed to savour of Puritanism. The author, however, published another edition in 1610; indeed, he seems to have had a fondness for this style of work; for in 1604 he published a dull poem, Moyses in a Map of his Miracles, re-issued in 1630 as Moses his Birth and Miracles.

Accompanying this piece, in 1630, were two other 'Divine poems': Noah's Floud, and David and Goliath. Noah's Floud is, in part, one of Drayton's happiest attempts at the catalogue style of bestiary; and Mr. Elton finds in it some foreshadowing of the manner of Paradise Lost. But, as a whole, Drayton's attempts in this direction deserve the oblivion into which they, in common with the similar productions of other authors, have fallen. In the dedication and preface to the Harmony of the Church are some of the few traces of Euphuism shown in Drayton's work; passages in the Heroical Epistles also occur to the mind He was always averse to affectation, literary or otherwise, and in Elegy VIII deliberately condemns Lyly's fantastic style.

Probably before Drayton went up to London, Sir Henry Goodere saw that he would stand in need of a patron more powerful than the master of Polesworth, and introduced him to the Earl and Countess of Bedford. Those who believe Drayton to have been a Pope in petty spite, identify the 'Idea' of his earlier poems with Lucy, Countess of Bedford; though they are forced to acknowledge as self-evident that the 'Idea' of his later work is Anne, Lady Raynsford. They then proceed to say that Drayton, after consistently honouring the Countess in his verse for twelve years, abruptly transferred his allegiance, not forgetting to heap foul abuse on his former patroness, out of pique at some temporary withdrawal of favour. Not only is this directly contrary to all we know and can infer of Drayton's character, but Mr. Elton has decisively disproved it by a summary of bibliographical and other evidence. Into the question it is here unnecessary to enter, and it has been mentioned only because it alone, of the many Drayton-controversies, has cast any slur on the poet's reputation.

In 1593, Drayton published Idea, the Shepherds Garland, in nine Eclogues; in 1606 he added a tenth, the best of all, to the new edition, and rearranged the order, so that the new eclogue became the ninth. In these Pastorals, while following the Shepherds Calendar in many ways, he already displays something of the sturdy independence which characterized him through life. He abandons Spenser's quasi-rustic dialect, and, while keeping to most of the pastoral conventions, such as the singing-match and threnody, he contrives to introduce something of a more natural and homely strain. He keeps the political allusions, notably in the Eclogue containing the song in praise of Beta, who is, of course, Queen Elizabeth. But an over-bold remark in the last line of that song was struck out in 1606; and the new eclogue has no political reference. He is not ashamed to allude directly to Spenser; and indeed his direct debts are limited to a few scattered phrases, as in the Ballad of Dowsabel. Almost to the end of his literary career, Drayton mentions Spenser with reverence and praise.

It is in the songs interspersed in the Eclogues that Drayton's best work at this time is to be found: already his metrical versatility is discernible; for though he doubtless remembered the many varieties of metre employed by Spenser in the Calendar, his verses already bear a stamp of their own. The long but impetuous lines, such as 'Trim up her golden tresses with Apollo's sacred tree', afford a striking contrast to the archaic romance-metre, derived from Sir Thopas and its fellows, which appears in Dowsabel, and it again to the melancholy, murmuring cadences of the lament for Elphin. It must, however, be confessed that certain of the songs in the 1593 edition were full of recondite conceits and laboured antitheses, and were rightly struck out, to be replaced by lovelier poems, in the edition of 1606. The song to Beta was printed in Englands Helicon, 1600; here, for the first time, appeared the song of Dead Love, and for the only time, Rowlands Madrigal. In these songs, Drayton offends least in grammar, always a weak point with him; in the body of the Eclogues, in the earlier Sonnets, in the Odes, occur the most extraordinary and perplexing inversions. Quite the most striking feature of the Eclogues, especially in their later form, is their bold attempt at greater realism, at a breaking-away from the conventional images and scenery.

Having paid his tribute to one poetic fashion, Drayton in 1594 fell in with the prevailing craze for sonneteering, and published Ideas Mirrour, a series of fifty-one 'amours' or sonnets, with two prefatory poems, one by Drayton and one by an unknown, signing himself Gorbo il fidele. The title of these poems Drayton possibly borrowed from the French sonneteer, de Pontoux: in their style much recollection of Sidney, Constable, and Daniel is traceable. They are ostensibly addressed to his mistress, and some of them are genuine in feeling; but many are merely imitative exercises in conceit; some, apparently, trials in metre. These amours were again printed, with the title of 'sonnets', in 1599, 1600, 1602, 1603, 1605, 1608, 1610, 1613, 1619, and 1631, during the poet's lifetime. It is needless here to discuss whether Drayton were the 'rival poet' to Shakespeare, whether these sonnets were really addressed to a man, or merely to the ideal Platonic beauty; for those who are interested in these points, I subjoin references to the sonnets which touch upon them. From the prentice-work evident in many of the Amours, it would seem that certain of them are among Drayton's earliest poems; but others show a craftsman not meanly advanced in his art. Nevertheless, with few exceptions, this first 'bundle of sonnets' consists rather of trials of skill, bubbles of the mind; most of his sonnets which strike the reader as touched or penetrated with genuine passion belong to the editions from 1599 onwards; implying that his love for Anne Goodere, if at all represented in these poems, grew with his years, for the 'love-parting' is first found in the edition of 1619. But for us the question should not be, are these sonnets genuine representations of the personal feeling of the poet? but rather, how far do they arouse or echo in us as individuals the universal passion? There are at least some of Drayton's sonnets which possess a direct, instant, and universal appeal, by reason of their simple force and straightforward ring; and not in virtue of any subtle charm of sound and rhythm, or overmastering splendour of diction or thought. Ornament vanishes, and soberness and simplicity increase, as we proceed in the editions of the sonnets. Drayton's chief attempt in the jewelled or ornamental style appeared in 1595, with the title of Endimion and Phoebe, and was, in a sense, an imitation of Marlowe's Hero and Leander. Hero and Leander is, as Swinburne says, a shrine of Parian marble, illumined from within by a clear flame of passion; while Endimion and Phoebe is rather a curiously wrought tapestry, such as that in Mortimer's Tower, woven in splendid and harmonious colours, wherein, however, the figures attain no clearness or subtlety of outline, and move in semi-conventional scenery. It is, none the less, graceful and impressive, and of a like musical fluency with other poems of its class, such as Venus and Adonis, or Salmacis and Hermaphrodius. Parts of it were re-set and spoilt in a 1606 publication of Drayton's, called The Man in the Moone.

In 1593 and 1594 Drayton also published his earliest pieces on the mediaeval theme of the 'Falls of the Illustrious'; they were Peirs Gavesson and Matilda the faire and chaste daughter of the Lord Robert Fitzwater. Here Drayton followed in the track of Boccaccio, Lydgate, and the Mirrour for Magistrates, walking in the way which Chaucer had derided in his Monkes Tale: and with only too great fidelity does Drayton adapt himself to the dullnesses of his model: fine rhetoric is not altogether wanting, and there is, of course, the consciousness that these subjects deal with the history of his beloved country, but neither these, nor Robert, Duke of Normandy (1596), nor Great Cromwell, Earl of Essex (1607 and 1609), nor the Miseries of Margaret (1627) can escape the charge of tediousness. England's Heroical Epistles were first published in 1597, and other editions, of 1598, 1599, and 1602, contain new epistles. These are Drayton's first attempt to strike out a new and original vein of English poetry: they are a series of letters, modelled on Ovid's Heroides, addressed by various pairs of lovers, famous in English history, to each other, and arranged in chronological order, from Henry II and Rosamond to Lady Jane Grey and Lord Guilford Dudley. They are, in a sense, the most important of Drayton's writings, and they have certainly been the most popular, up to the early nineteenth century. In these poems Drayton foreshadowed, and probably inspired, the smooth style of Fairfax, Waller, and Dryden. The metre, the grammar, and the thought, are all perfectly easy to follow, even though he employs many of the Ovidian 'turns' and 'clenches'. A certain attempt at realization of the different characters is observable, but the poems are fine rhetorical exercises rather than realizations of the dramatic and passionate possibilities of their themes. In 1596, Drayton, as we have seen, published the Mortimeriados, a kind of epic, with Mortimer as its hero, of the wars between King Edward II and the Barons. It was written in the seven-line stanza of Chaucer's Troilus and Cressida and Spenser's Hymns. On its republication in 1603, with the title of the Barons' Wars, the metre was changed to ottava rima, and Drayton showed, in an excellent preface, that he fully appreciated the principles and the subtleties of the metrical art. While possessing many fine passages, the Barons' Wars is somewhat dull, lacking much of the poetry of the older version; and does not escape from Drayton's own criticism of Daniel's Chronicle Poems: 'too much historian in verse, ... His rhymes were smooth, his metres well did close, But yet his manner better fitted prose'. The description of Mortimer's Tower in the sixth book recalls the ornate style of Endimion and Phoebe, while the fifth book, describing the miseries of King Edward, is the most moving and dramatic. But there is a general lifelessness and lack of movement for which these purple passages barely atone. The cause of the production of so many chronicle poems about this time has been supposed to be the desire of showing the horrors of civil war, at a time when the queen was growing old, and no successor had, as it seemed, been accepted. Also they were a kind of parallel to the Chronicle Play; and Drayton, in any case even if we grant him to have been influenced by the example of Daniel, never needed much incentive to treat a national theme.

About this time, we find Drayton writing for the stage. It seems unnecessary here to discuss whether the writing of plays is evidence of Drayton's poverty, or his versatility; but the fact remains that he had a hand in the production of about twenty. Of these, the only one which certainly survives is The first part of the true and honorable historie, of the life of Sir John Oldcastle, the good Lord Cobham, &c. It is practically impossible to distinguish Drayton's share in this curious play, and it does not, therefore, materially assist the elucidation of the question whether he had any dramatic feeling or skill. It can be safely affirmed that the dramatic instinct was nor uppermost in his mind; he was a Seneca rather than a Euripides: but to deny him all dramatic idea, as does Dr. Whitaker, is too severe. There is decided, if slender, dramatic skill and feeling in certain of the Nymphals. Drayton's persons are usually, it must be said, rather figures in a tableau, or series of tableaux; but in the second and seventh Nymphals, and occasionally in the tenth, there is real dramatic movement. Closely connected with this question is the consideration of humour, which is wrongly denied to Drayton. Humour is observable first, perhaps, in the Owle (1604); then in the Ode to his Rival (1619); and later in the Nymphidia, Shepheards Sirena, and Muses Elyzium. The second Nymphal shows us the quiet laughter, the humorous twinkle, with which Drayton writes at times. The subject is an [Greek: agôn] or contest between two shepherds for the affections of a nymph called Lirope: Lalus is a vale-bred swain, of refined and elegant manners, skilled, nevertheless, in all manly sports and exercises; Cleon, no less a master in physical prowess, was nurtured by a hind in the mountains; the contrast between their manners is admirably sustained: Cleon is rough, inclined to be rude and scoffing, totally without tact, even where his mistress is concerned. Lalus remembers her upbringing and her tastes; he makes no unnecessary or ostentatious display of wealth; his gifts are simple and charming, while Cleon's are so grotesquely unsuited to a swain, that it is tempting to suppose that Drayton was quietly satirizing Marlowe's Passionate Shepherd. Lirope listens gravely to the swains in turn, and makes demure but provoking answers, raising each to the height of hope, and then casting them both down into the depths of despair; finally she refuses both, yet without altogether killing hope. Her first answer is a good specimen of her banter and of Drayton's humour.

On the accession of James I, Drayton hastened to greet the King with a somewhat laboured song To the Maiestie of King James; but this poem was apparently considered to be premature: he cried Vivat Rex, without having said, Mortua est eheu Regina, and accordingly he suffered the penalty of his 'forward pen', and was severely neglected by King and Court. Throughout James's reign a darker and more satirical mood possesses Drayton, intruding at times even into his strenuous recreation-ground, the Poly-Olbion, and manifesting itself more directly in his satires, the Owle (1604), the Moon-Calfe (1627), the Man in the Moone (1606), and his verse-letters and elegies; while his disappointment with the times, the country, and the King, flashes out occasionally even in the Odes, and is heard in his last publication, the Muses Elizium (1630). To counterbalance the disappointment in his hopes from the King, Drayton found a new and life-long friend in Walter Aston, of Tixall, in Staffordshire; this gentleman was created Knight of the Bath by James, and made Drayton one of his esquires. By Aston's 'continual bounty' the poet was able to devote himself almost entirely to more congenial literary work; for, while Meres speaks of the Poly-Olbion in 1598, and we may easily see that Drayton had the idea of that work at least as early as 1594, yet he cannot have been able to give much time to it till now. Nevertheless, the 'declining and corrupt times' worked on Drayton's mind and grieved and darkened his soul, for we must remember that he was perfectly prosperous then and was not therefore incited to satire by bodily want or distress.

In 1604 he published the Owle, a mild satire, under the form of a moral fable of government, reminding the reader a little of the Parlement of Foules. The Man in the Moone (1606) is partly a recension of Endimion and Phoebe, but is a heterogeneous mass of weakly satire, of no particular merit. The Moon-Calfe (1627) is Drayton's most savage and misanthropic excursion into the region of Satire; in which, though occasionally nobly ironic, he is more usually coarse and blustering, in the style of Marston. In 1605 Drayton brought out his first 'collected poems', from which the Eclogues and the Owle are omitted; and in 1606 he published his Poemes Lyrick and Pastorall, Odes, Eglogs, The Man in the Moone. Of these the Eglogs are a recension of the Shepherd's Garland of 1593: we have already spoken of The Man in the Moone. The Odes are by far the most important and striking feature of the book. In the preface, Drayton professes to be following Pindar, Anacreon, and Horace, though, as he modestly implies, at a great distance. Under the title of Odes he includes a variety of subjects, and a variety of metres; ranging from an Ode to his Harp or to his Criticks, to a Ballad of Agincourt, or a poem on the Rose compared with his Mistress. In the edition of 1619 appeared several more Odes, including some of the best; while many of the others underwent careful revision, notably the Ballad. 'Sing wee the Rose,' perhaps because of its unintelligibility, and the Ode to his friend John Savage, perhaps because too closely imitated from Horace, were omitted. Drayton was not the first to use the term Ode for a lyrical poem, in English: Soothern in 1584, and Daniel in 1592 had preceded him; but he was the first to give the name popularity in England, and to lift the kind as Ronsard had lifted it in France; and till the time of Cowper no other English poet showed mastery of the short, staccato measure of the Anacreontic as distinct from the Pindaric Ode. In the Odes Drayton shows to the fullest extent his metrical versatility: he touches the Skeltonic metre, the long ten-syllabled line of the Sacrifice to Apollo; and ascends from the smooth and melodious rhythms of the New Year through the inspiring harp-tones of the Virginian Voyage to the clangour and swing of the Ballad of Agincourt. His grammar is possibly more distorted here than anywhere, but, as Mr. Elton says, 'these are the obstacles of any poet who uses measures of four or six syllables.' His tone throughout is rather that of the harp, as played, perhaps, in Polesworth Hall, than that of any other instrument; but in 1619 Drayton has taken to him the lute of Carew and his compeers. In 1619 the style is lighter, the fancy gayer, more exquisite, more recondite. Most of his few metaphysical conceits are to be found in these later Odes, as in the Heart, the Valentine, and the Crier. In the comparison of the two editions the nobler, if more strained, tone of the earlier is obvious; it is still Elizabethan, in its nobility of ideal and purpose, in its enthusiasm, in its belief and confidence in England and her men; and this even though we catch a glimpse of the Jacobean woe in the Ode to John Savage: the 1619 Odes are of a different world; their spirit is lighter, more insouciant in appearance, though perhaps studiedly so; the rhythms are more fantastic, with less of strength and firmness, though with more of grace and superficial beauty; even the very textual alterations, while usually increasing the grace and the music of the lines, remind the reader that something of the old spontaneity and freshness is gone.

In 1607 and 1609, Drayton published two editions of the last and weakest of his mediaeval poems—the Legend of Great Cromwell; and for the next few years he produced nothing new, only attending to the publication of certain reprints and new editions. During this time, however, he was working steadily at the Poly-Olbion, helped by the patronage of Aston and of Prince Henry. In 1612-13, Drayton burst upon an indifferent world with the first part of the great poem, containing eighteen songs; the title-page will give the best idea of the contents and plan of the book: 'Poly-Olbion or a Chorographicall Description of the Tracts, Rivers, Mountaines, Forests, and other Parts of this renowned Isle of Great Britaine, With intermixture of the most Remarquable Stories, Antiquities, Wonders, Rarityes, Pleasures, and Commodities of the same: Digested in a Poem by Michael Drayton, Esq. With a Table added, for direction to those occurrences of Story and Antiquities, whereunto the Course of the Volume easily leades not.' &c. On this work Drayton had been engaged for nearly the whole of his poetical career. The learning and research displayed in the poem are extraordinary, almost equalling the erudition of Selden in his Annotations to each Song. The first part was, for various reasons, a drug in the market, and Drayton found great difficulty in securing a publisher for the second part. But during the years from 1613 to 1622, he became acquainted with Drummond of Hawthornden through a common friend, Sir William Alexander of Menstry, afterwards Earl of Stirling. In 1618, Drayton starts a correspondence; and towards the end of the year mentions that he is corresponding also with Andro Hart, bookseller, of Edinburgh. The subject of his letter was probably the publication of the Second Part; which Drayton alludes to in a letter of 1619 thus: 'I have done twelve books more, that is from the eighteenth book, which was Kent, if you note it; all the East part and North to the river Tweed; but it lies by me; for the booksellers and I are in terms; they are a company of base knaves, whom I both scorn and kick at.' Finally, in 1622, Drayton got Marriott, Grismand, and Dewe, of London, to take the work, and it was published with a dedication to Prince Charles, who, after his brother's death, had given Drayton patronage. Drayton's preface to the Second Part is well worth quoting:

'To any that will read it. When I first undertook this Poem, or, as some very skilful in this kind have pleased to term it, this Herculean labour, I was by some virtuous friends persuaded, that I should receive much comfort and encouragement therein; and for these reasons; First, that it was a new, clear, way, never before gone by any; then, that it contained all the Delicacies, Delights, and Rarities of this renowned Isle, interwoven with the Histories of the Britons, Saxons, Normans, and the later English: And further that there is scarcely any of the Nobility or Gentry of this land, but that he is in some way or other by his Blood interested therein. But it hath fallen out otherwise; for instead of that comfort, which my noble friends (from the freedom of their spirits) proposed as my due, I have met with barbarous ignorance, and base detraction; such a cloud hath the Devil drawn over the world's judgment, whose opinion is in few years fallen so far below all ballatry, that the lethargy is incurable: nay, some of the Stationers, that had the selling of the First Part of this Poem, because it went not so fast away in the sale, as some of their beastly and abominable trash, (a shame both to our language and nation) have either despitefully left out, or at least carelessly neglected the

Epistles to the Readers, and so have cozened the buyers with unperfected books; which these that have undertaken the Second Part, have been forced to amend in the First, for the small number that are yet remaining in their hands. And some of our outlandish, unnatural, English, (I know not how otherwise to express them) stick not to say that there is nothing in this Island worth studying for, and take a great pride to be ignorant in any thing thereof; for these, since they delight in their folly, I wish it may be hereditary from them to their posterity, that their children may be begg'd for fools to the fifth generation, until it may be beyond the memory of man to know that there was ever other of their families: neither can this deter me from going on with Scotland, if means and time do not hinder me, to perform as much as I have promised in my First Song:

Till through the sleepy main, to Thuly I have gone,
And seen the Frozen Isles, the cold Deucalidon,
Amongst whose iron Rocks, grim Saturn yet remains
Bound in those gloomy caves with adamantine chains.

And as for those cattle whereof I spake before, Odi profanum vulgus, et arceo, of which I account them, be they never so great, and so I leave them. To my friends, and the lovers of my labours, I wish all happiness.
Michael Drayton.'

The Poly-Olbion as a whole is easy and pleasant to read; and though in some parts it savours too much of a mere catalogue, yet it has many things truly poetical. The best books are perhaps the XIII, XIV and XV, where he is on his own ground, and therefore naturally at his best. It is interesting to notice how much attention and space he devotes to Wales. He describes not only the 'wonders' but also the fauna and flora of each district; and of the two it would seem that the flowers interested him more. Though he was a keen observer of country sights and sounds (a fact sufficiently attested by the Nymphidia and the Nymphals), it is evident that his interest in most things except flowers was rather momentary or conventional than continuous and heart-felt; but of the flowers he loves to talk, whether he weaves us a garland for the Thame's wedding, or gives us the contents of a maund of simples; and his love, if somewhat homely and unimaginative, is apparent enough. But the main inspiration, as it is the main theme, of the Poly-Olbion is the glory and might and wealth, past, present, and future, of England, her possessions and her folk. Through all this glory, however, we catch the tone of Elizabethan sorrow over the 'Ruines of Time'; grief that all these mighty men and their works will perish and be forgotten, unless the poet makes them live for ever on the lips of men. Drayton's own voluminousness has defeated his purpose, and sunk his poem by its own bulk. Though it is difficult to go so far as Mr. Bullen, and say that the only thing better than a stroll in the Poly-Olbion is one in a Sussex lane, it is still harder to agree with Canon Beeching, that 'there are few beauties on the road', the beauties are many, though of a quietly rural type, and the road, if long and winding, is of good surface, while its cranks constitute much of its charm. It is doubtless, from the outside, an appalling poem in these days of epitomes and monographs, but it certainly deserves to be rescued from oblivion and read.

In 1618 Drayton contributed two Elegies to Henry FitzGeoffrey's Satyrs and Epigrames. These were on the Lady Penelope Clifton, and on 'the death of the three sonnes of the Lord Sheffield, drowned neere where Trent falleth into Humber'. Neither is remarkable save for far-fetched conceits; they were reprinted in 1610, and again, with many others, in the volume of 1627. In 1619 Drayton issued a folio collected edition of his works, and reprinted it in 1620. In 1627 followed a folio of wholly fresh matter, including the Battaile of Agincourt; the Miseries of Queene Margarite, Nimphidia, Quest of Cinthia, Shepheards Sirena, Moone-Calfe, and Elegies upon sundry occasions. The Battaile of Agincourt is a somewhat otiose expansion, with purple patches, of the Ballad; it is, nevertheless, Drayton's best lengthy piece on a historical theme. Of the Miseries of Queene Margarite and of the

Moone-Calfe we have already spoken. The most notable piece in the book is the Nimphidia. This poem of the Court of Fairy has 'invention, grace, and humour', as Canon Beeching has said. It would be interesting to know exactly when it was composed and committed to paper, for it is thought that the three fairy poems in Herrick's Hesperides were written about 1626. In any case, Drayton's poem touches very little, and chiefly in the beginning, on the subject of any one of Herrick's three pieces. The style, execution, and impression left on the reader are quite different; even as they are totally unlike those of the Midsummer Night's Dream. Herrick's pieces are extraordinary combinations of the idea of 'King of Shadows', with a reality fantastically sober: the poems are steeped in moonlight. In Drayton all is clear day, or the most unromantic of nights; though everything is charming, there is no attempt at idealization, little of the higher faculty of imagination; but great realism, and much play of fancy. Herrick's verses were written by Cobweb and Moth together, Drayton's by Puck. Granting, however, the initial deficiency in subtlety of charm, the whole poem is inimitably graceful and piquant. The gay humour, the demure horror of the witchcraft, the terrible seriousness of the battle, wonderfully realize the mock-heroic gigantesque; and while there is not the minute accuracy of Gulliver in Lilliput, Drayton did not write for a sceptical or too-prying audience; quite half his readers believed more or less in fairies. In the metre of the poem Drayton again echoes that of the older romances, as he did in Dowsabel. In the Quest of Cinthia, while ostensibly we come to the real world of mortals, we are really in a non-existent land of pastoral convention, in the most pseudo-Arcadian atmosphere in which Drayton ever worked. The metre and the language are, however, charmingly managed. The Shepheards Sirena is a poem, apparently, 'where more is meant than meets the ear,' as so often in pastoral poetry; it is difficult to see exactly what is meant; but the Jacobean strain of doubt and fear is there, and the poem would seem to have been written some time earlier than 1627. The Elegies comprise a great variety of styles and themes; some are really threnodies, some verse-letters, some laments over the evil times, and one a summary of Drayton's literary opinions. He employs the couplet in his Elegies with a masterly hand, often with a deliberately rugged effect, as in his broader Marstonic satire addressed to William Browne; while the line of greater smoothness but equal strength is to be seen in the letters to Sandys and Jeffreys. He is fantastic and conceited in most of the threnodies; but, as is natural, that on his old friend, Sir Henry Raynsford, is least artificial and fullest of true feeling. The epistle to Henery Reynolds. Of Poets and Poesie shows Drayton as a sane and sagacious critic, ready to see the good, but keen to discern the weakness also; perhaps the clearest evidence of his critical skill is the way in which nearly all of his judgements on his contemporaries coincide with the received modern opinions.

In his later years Drayton enjoyed the patronage of the third Earl and Countess of Dorset; and in 1630 he published his last volume, the Muses Elizium, of which he dedicated the pastoral part to the Earl, and the three divine poems at the end to the Countess. The Muses Elizium proper consists of Ten Pastorals or Nymphals, prefaced by a Description of Elizium. The three divine poems have been mentioned before, and were Noah's Floud, Moses his Birth and Miracles, and David and Goliah. The Nymphals are the crown and summary of much of the best in Drayton's work. Here he departed from the conventional type of pastoral, even more than in the Shepherd's Garland; but to say that he sang of English rustic life would hardly be true: the sixth Nymphal, allowing for a few pardonable exaggerations by the competitors, is almost all English, if we except the names; so is the tenth with the same exception; the first and fourth might take place anywhere, but are not likely in any country; the second is more conventional; the fifth is almost, but not quite, English; the third, seventh, and ninth are avowedly classical in theme; while the eighth is a more delicate and subtle fairy poem than the Nymphidia. The fourth and tenth Nymphals are also touched with the sadder, almost satiric vein; the former inveighing against the English imitation of foreigners and love of extravagance in dress; while the tenth complains of the improvident and wasteful felling of trees in the English forests. This last Nymphal, though designedly an epilogue, is probably rather a warning than a despairing lament, even though we conceive the old satyr to be Drayton himself. As a whole the Nymphals show Drayton at his happiest and lightest in style and metre; at his moments of greatest serenity and even gaiety; an atmosphere of sunshine seems to envelope them all, though the sun sink behind a cloud in the last. His music now is that of a rippling stream, whereas in his earlier days he spoke weightier and more sonorous words, with a mouth of gold.

To estimate the poetical faculty of Drayton is a somewhat perplexing task; for, while rarely subtle, or rising to empyrean heights, he wrote in such varied styles, on such various themes, that the task, at first, seems that of criticizing many poets, not one. But through all his work runs the same eminently English spirit, the same honesty and clearness of idea, the same stolidity of purpose, and not infrequently of execution also; the same enthusiasm characterizes all his earlier, and much of his later work; the enthusiasm especially characteristic of Elizabethan England, and shown by Drayton in his passion for England and the English, in his triumphant joy in their splendid past, and his certainty of their future glory. As a poet, he lacked imagination and fine fury; he supplied their place by the airiest and clearest of fancies, by the strenuous labour of a great brain illumined by the steady flame of love for his country and for his lady. Mr. Courthope has said that he lacked loftiness and resolution of artistic purpose; without these, we ask, how could a man, not lavishly dowered with poetry in his soul, have achieved so much of it? It was his very fixity and loftiness of purpose, his English stubbornness and doggedness of resolution that enabled him to surmount so many obstacles of style and metre, of subject and thought. His two purposes, of glorifying his mistress and his friends, and of sounding England's glories past and future, while insisting on the dangers of a present decadence, never flagged or failed. All his poetry up to 1627 has this object directly or secondarily; and much after this date. Of the more abstract and universal aspects of his art he had not much conception; but he caught eagerly at the fashionable belief in the eternizing power of poetry; and had it not been that, where his patriotism was uppermost, he was deficient in humour and sense of proportion, he would have succeeded better: as it is, his more directly patriotic pieces are usually the dullest or longest of his works. He requires, like all other poets, the impulse of an absolutely personal and individual feeling, a moment of more intimate sympathy, to rouse him to his heights of song. Thus the Ballad of Agincourt is on the very theme of all patriotic themes that most attracted him; Virginian and other Voyages lay very close to his heart; and in certain sonnets to his lady lies his only imperishable work. Of sheer melody and power of song he had little, apart from his themes: he could not have sat down and written a few lark's or nightingale's notes about nothing as some of his contemporaries were able to do: he required the stimulus of a subject, and if he were really moved thereby he beat the music out. Only in one or two of the later Odes, and in the volumes of 1627 and 1630, does his music ever seem to flow from him naturally. Akin to this quality of broad and extensive workmanship, to this faculty of taking a subject and when writing, with all thought concentrated on it, rather than on the method of writing about it, is his strange lack of what are usually called 'quotations'. For this is not only due to the fact that he is little known; there are, besides, so few detached remarks or aphorisms that are separately quotable; so few examples of that curiosa felicitas of diction: lines like these,

Thy Bowe, halfe broke, is peec'd with old desire;
Her Bowe is beauty with ten thousand strings....

are rare enough. Drayton, in fact, comes as near controverting the statement Poeta nascitur, non fit, as any one in English literature: by diligent toil and earnest desire he won a place for himself in the second rank of English poets: through love he once set foot in the circle of the mightiest. Sincere he was always, simple often, sensuous rarely. His great industry, his careful study, and his great receptivity are shown in the unusual spectacle of a man who has sung well in the language of his youth, suddenly learning, in his age, the tongue spoken by the younger generation, and reproducing it with individuality and sureness of touch. It is in rhetoric, splendid or rugged, in argument, in plain statement or description, in the outline sketch of a picture, that Drayton excels; magic of atmosphere and colouring are rarely present. Stolidity is, perhaps, his besetting sin; yet it is the sign of a slow, not a dull, intellect; an intellect, like his heart, which never let slip what it had once taken to itself.

As a man Drayton would seem to have been an excellent type of the sturdy, clear-headed, but yet romantic and enthusiastic Englishman; gifted with much natural ability, sedulously increased by study; quietly humorous, self-restrained; and if temporarily soured by disappointment and the disjointed times, yet emerging at last into a greater serenity, a more unadulterated gaiety than had ever before characterized him. It is possible, but from his clear and sane balance of mind improbable, that many of his light later poems are due to deliberate self-blinding and self-deception, a walking in enchanted lands of the mind.

Of Drayton's three known portraits the earliest shows him at the age of thirty-six, and is now in the National Portrait Gallery. A look of quiet, speculative melancholy seems to pervade it; there is, as yet, no moroseness, no evidence of severe conflict with the world, no shadow of stress or of doubt. The second and best-known portrait shows us Drayton at the age of fifty, and was engraved by Hole, as a frontispiece to the poems of 1619. Here a notable change has come over the face; the mouth is hardened, and depressed at the corners through disappointment and disillusionment; the eyes are full of a pathos increased by the puzzled and perturbed uplift of the brows. Yet a stubbornness and tenacity of purpose invests the features and reminds us that Drayton is of the old and sound Elizabethan stock, 'on evil days though fallen.' Let it be remembered, that he was in 1613, when the portrait was taken, in more or less prosperous circumstances; it was the sad degeneracy, the meanness and feebleness of the generation around him, that chiefly depressed and embittered him. The final portrait, now in the Dulwich Gallery, represents the poet as a man of sixty-five; and is quite in keeping with the sunnier and calmer tone of his later poetry. It is the face of one who has not emerged unscathed from the world's conflict, but has attained to a certain calm, a measure of tranquillity, a portion of content, who has learnt the lesson that there is a soul of goodness in things evil. The Hole portrait shows him with long hair, small 'goatee' beard, and aquiline nose drawn up at the nostrils: while the National portrait shows a type of nose and beard intermediate between the Hole and the Dulwich pictures: the general contour of the face, though the forehead is broad enough, is long and oval. Drayton seems to have been tall and thin, and to have been very susceptible of cold, and therefore to have hated Winter and the North. He is said to have shared in the supper which caused Shakespeare's death; but his own verses breathe the spirit of Milton's sonnet to Cyriack Skinner, rather than that of a devotee of Bacchus.

He died in 1631, probably December 23, and was buried under the North wall of Westminster Abbey. Meres's opinion of his character during his early life is as follows: 'As Aulus Persius Flaccus is reported among al writers to be of an honest life and upright conuersation: so Michael Drayton, quem totics honoris et amoris causa nomino, among schollers, souldiours, Poets, and all sorts of people is helde for a man of uertuous disposition, honest conversation, and well governed cariage; which is almost miraculous among good wits in these declining and corrupt times, when there is nothing but rogery in villanous man, and when cheating and craftines is counted the cleanest wit, and soundest wisedome.' Fuller also, in a similar strain, says, 'He was a pious poet, his conscience having the command of his fancy, very temperate in his life, slow of speech, and inoffensive in company.'

A Chronology of Michael Drayton's Life and Works

c. 1574	Anne Goodere born
February, 1591	Drayton in London. Harmony of Church.
1593	Idea, the Shepherd's Garland. Legend of Peirs Gaveston.
1594	Ideas Mirrour. Matilda. Lucy Harrington becomes Countess of Bedford.
1595	Sir Henry Goodere the elder dies. Endimion and Phoebe, dedicated to Lucy Bedford.
1595-6	Anne Goodere married to Sir Henry Raynsford.
1596	Mortimeriados. Legends of Robert, Matilda, and Gaveston.
1597	England's Heroical Epistles.
1598	Drayton already at work on the Poly-Olbion.
1599	Epistles and Idea sonnets, new edition. (Date of Drayton portrait in National Portrait Gallery.)
1600	Sir John Oldcastle.
1602	New edition of Epistles and Idea.
1603	Drayton made an Esquire of the Bath, to Sir Walter Aston. To the Maiestie of King James. Barons' Wars.
1604	The Owle. A Pean Triumphall. Moyses in a Map of his Miracles.
1605	First collected edition of Poems. Another edition of Idea and Epistles.
1606	Poemes Lyrick and Pastorall. Odes. Eglogs. The Man in the Moone.
1607	Legend of Great Cromwell.
1608	Reprint of Collected Poems.
1609	Another edition of Cromwell.
1610	Reprint of Collected Poems.
1613	Reprint of Collected Poems. First Part of Poly-Olbion.
1618	Two Elegies in FitzGeoffrey's Satyrs and Epigrames.
1619	Collected Folio edition of Poems.
1620	Second edition of Elegies, and reprint of 1619 Poems.
1622	Poly-Olbion complete.
1627	Battle of Agincourt, Nymphidia, &c.
1630	Muses Elizium. Noah's Floud. Moses his Birth and Miracles. David and Goliah.
1631	Second edition of 1627 folio. Drayton dies December 23rd.
1636	Posthumous poem appeared in Annalia Dubrensia.
1637	Poems.

Michael Drayton – A Concise Bibliography

The Major Works

The Harmony of the Church (1591)
Idea, The Shepherd's Garland (1593)
Idea's Mirror (1594)
Peirs Gaveston (1593 or 1594)
Matilda (1594)
Endimion and Phoebe: Idea's Latmus (1595)
The Tragical Legend of Robert, Duke of Normandy (1596)
Mortimeriados (1596)
England's Heroicall Epistles (1597)
The First Part of the Life of Sir John Oldcastle (1600)
The Barons' Wars in the Reign of Edward II (1603)
The Owl (1604)

The Man in the Moon (1606)
The Legend of Thomas Cromwell, Earl of Essex (1607)
Poly-Olbion (1612 & 1622)
Idea (1619)
Pastorals: Containing Eclogues (1619)
Odes (1619)
The Battle of Agincourt (published 1627)
The Quest of Cynthia (published 1627)
Elegies Upon Sundry Occasions (1627)
Nymphidia, the Court of Fairy (1627)
The Shepherd's Sirena (1627)
Muses' Elysium (1630)
Moses' Birth and Miracles (1630)

www.ingramcontent.com/pod-product-compliance
Lightning Source LLC
Chambersburg PA
CBHW060147050426
42448CB00010B/2343